In *Improving Instruction Together*, Steve Ventura offers school leaders a comprehensive and valuable road map for meaningful collaboration. His Achievement Teams framework provides the structured protocols needed to transform teacher teams into engines of instructional excellence. What sets this work apart is Ventura's deep understanding of how effective leadership drives student achievement through purposeful data analysis, strategic goal setting, and research-based instructional strategies. This essential resource will help educational leaders create the conditions where teachers thrive collectively—and students benefit immeasurably.

Nathan Lang-Raad
educator, author, speaker

Improving Instruction Together is a powerful call to action for educational leaders seeking to deepen collaboration and raise student achievement. With clarity, research, and real-world stories, Steve Ventura offers a practical framework that empowers leaders at all levels to transform teacher teams into high-impact collectives. This book goes beyond theory and provides tools, strategies, and reflection prompts that inspire leaders to model the instructional excellence they wish to see. This book is a must-read for any educator committed to building schools where collaboration, clarity, and accountability drive sustained student success.

Eric Sheninger
author, thought leader, innovator, educator, speaker

If we want teachers to build student agency into the culture of their classrooms and have students learn together, set personal goals, and reflect on how to improve their performance, then we need school leaders to nurture teachers and coaches in similar ways. *Improving Instruction Together* brilliantly weaves together current research and actionable strategies with opportunities for teachers to take the time to be reflective while learning and expanding their collective skills and knowledge. This book is a must-have guide for today's educational leaders.

Karin Hess
president, Educational Research in Action, LLC

Improving Instruction TOGETHER

Many ASCD members received
this book as a member benefit
upon its initial release.

Learn more at
www.ascd.org/memberbooks.

Other ASCD publications by Steve Ventura:

Achievement Teams: How a Better Approach to PLCs Can Improve Student Outcomes and Teacher Efficacy with Michelle Ventura

Highly Effective PLCs and Teacher Teams (Quick Reference Guide for Leaders) with Michelle Ventura

Improving Instruction Together

Leading Achievement Teams and PLCs

STEVE VENTURA

Arlington, Virginia USA

2111 Wilson Boulevard, Suite 300 • Arlington, VA 22201 USA
Phone: 800-933-2723 or 703-578-9600
Website: www.ascd.org • Email: member@ascd.org
Author guidelines: www.ascd.org/write

Richard Culatta, *Chief Executive Director;* Anthony Rebora, *Chief Content Officer;* Genny Ostertag, *Managing Director, Book Acquisitions and Editing;* Bill Varner, *Senior Acquisitions Editor;* Mary Beth Nielsen, *Director, Book Editing;* Jamie Greene, *Senior Editor;* Lisa Hill, *Graphic Designer;* Cynthia Stock, *Typesetter;* Kelly Marshall, *Production Manager;* Christopher Logan, *Senior Production Specialist;* Shajuan Martin, *E-Publishing Specialist*

Copyright © 2025 ASCD. All rights reserved. It is illegal to reproduce copies of this work in print or electronic format (including reproductions displayed on a secure intranet or stored in a retrieval system or other electronic storage device from which copies can be made or displayed) without the prior written permission of the publisher. By purchasing only authorized electronic or print editions and not participating in or encouraging piracy of copyrighted materials, you support the rights of authors and publishers. Readers who wish to reproduce or republish excerpts of this work in print or electronic format may do so for a small fee by contacting the Copyright Clearance Center (CCC), 222 Rosewood Dr., Danvers, MA 01923, USA (phone: 978-750-8400; fax: 978-646-8600; web: www.copyright.com). To inquire about site licensing options or any other reuse, contact ASCD Permissions at www.ascd.org/permissions or permissions@ascd.org. For a list of vendors authorized to license ASCD ebooks to institutions, see www.ascd.org/epubs. Send translation inquiries to translations@ascd.org.

ASCD® is a registered trademark of Association for Supervision and Curriculum Development. All other trademarks contained in this book are the property of, and reserved by, their respective owners, and are used for editorial and informational purposes only. No such use should be construed to imply sponsorship or endorsement of the book by the respective owners.

All web links in this book are correct as of the publication date below but may have become inactive or otherwise modified since that time. If you notice a deactivated or changed link, please email books@ascd.org with the words "Link Update" in the subject line. In your message, please specify the web link, the book title, and the page number on which the link appears.

PAPERBACK ISBN: 978-1-4166-3376-1   ASCD product #125034
PDF EBOOK ISBN: 978-1-4166-3377-8; see Books in Print for other formats.
Quantity discounts are available: email programteam@ascd.org or call 800-933-2723, ext. 5773, or 703-575-5773. For desk copies, go to www.ascd.org/deskcopy.

ASCD Member Book No. FY25-6 (Aug 2025 P). ASCD Member Books mail to Premium (P), Select (S), and Institutional Plus (I+) members on this schedule: Jan, PSI+; Feb, P; Apr, PSI+; May, P; Jul, PSI+; Aug, P; Sep, PSI+; Nov, PSI+; Dec, P. For current details on membership, see www.ascd.org/membership.

Library of Congress Cataloging-in-Publication Data
Names: Ventura, Steve author
Title: Improving instruction together : leading achievement teams and PLCs / Steve Ventura.
Description: Arlington, Virginia USA : ASCD, [2025] | Includes bibliographical references and index.
Identifiers: LCCN 2025013559 (print) | LCCN 2025013560 (ebook) | ISBN 9781416633761 paperback | ISBN 9781416633778 pdf
Subjects: LCSH: Teacher effectiveness | Professional learning communities | Teaching teams | Educational leadership
Classification: LCC LB1025.3 .V458 2025 (print) | LCC LB1025.3 (ebook)
LC record available at https://lccn.loc.gov/2025013559
LC ebook record available at https://lccn.loc.gov/2025013560

31 30 29 28 27 26 25   1 2 3 4 5 6 7 8 9 10 11 12

Improving Instruction Together

Preface ix

Chapter 1: The Collective Mindset 1

Chapter 2: Highly Effective Instructional Leadership 12

Chapter 3: The Leader's Role in Instructional Strategy Selection 28

Chapter 4: The Instructional Coach's Role in Teacher Teams and PLCs 51

Chapter 5: Indicators of Effective Collaboration 67

Chapter 6: Research-Driven Microteaching and Learning Labs 97

Chapter 7: Using Artificial Intelligence to Enhance Teacher Teams 108

Chapter 8: Putting It All Together 122

References 139

Index 143

About the Author 147

PREFACE

My Story

When I first became a principal, I wasn't ready. Sure, I was passionate about education, committed to my staff and students, and eager to make an impact. But when it came to instructional leadership—the kind of leadership that directly improves teaching and learning—I felt like an imposter. I stuck to what I knew: being visible, building relationships, and fostering school culture. These things mattered, but they weren't enough. Deep down, I knew I was playing it safe.

It wasn't until years later—after countless hours of research, collaboration, and learning alongside some of the best in the field—that I truly stepped into my role as an instructional leader. I finally understood that leadership isn't about managing a school; it's about leading a community of educators toward meaningful, lasting improvement. And that only happens when leaders at every level—principals, instructional coaches, teacher leaders, and district administrators—embrace collaboration, research-backed strategies, and a relentless focus on student success.

That's why I wrote this book. I want to save you from the uncertainty and hesitation I once felt. I want to give you the tools, mindsets, and frameworks I wish I had decades earlier. The strategies in this book are not theoretical; they're field-tested, practical, and designed for real educators facing real challenges.

How to Use This Book

As you explore each chapter, you'll notice an opening activity that explains why the chapter is important and how it can improve the application of collective leadership. Each chapter also concludes with a critical reflection activity. When both exercises are combined, you can assess your present standing with an opportunity to plan for the future. These activities are also appropriate for book studies, pulling and sharing quotes, action planning, and cross-chapter connections.

You'll also discover a number of QR codes, templates, instructional strategies, and leadership profiles that can enhance any school or district wishing to increase the overall efficiency of teacher and leader collaboration. Finally, the organization of this book allows for reader flexibility. For example, Chapter 1 builds a foundation, but the following chapters can be explored as standalone points of reference, depending on the needs of the reader.

A Solutions-Based Approach

The entire aim of this book is to help all educators cultivate a culture of teamwork, shared responsibility, and continuous improvement within their schools and districts. Throughout these pages, you'll find research-based insights, hands-on activities, and reflection prompts to help you assess where you are now and chart a path forward. Whether you're leading a school, coaching teachers, or shaping districtwide initiatives, you'll gain strategies to foster a culture of collaboration, drive instructional excellence, and create the kind of learning environment where both educators and students thrive.

Leadership is a journey, not a destination. My hope is that this book serves as a guide—one that accelerates your growth, sharpens your impact, and, most importantly, helps you lead with confidence, clarity, and purpose. Let's get started.

1

THE COLLECTIVE MINDSET

Unveiling the Collective

At the outset, you may find yourself asking, "What exactly is 'the collective'?" According to the dictionary, a *collective* is a cooperative ensemble or organization. From my perspective, though, in the context of education, the collective transcends a mere definition. It embodies an ethos wherein teachers, leaders, support staff, and additional community members converge around the unified ambition of fostering innovation, creativity, and expanded avenues for student success. It transcends the boundaries of individual teams or establishments to represent a group of educational professionals who are aligned in their vision of success, ensuring that objectives at the team, building, and district levels are universally understood and pursued.

As you navigate this book, the conversation will pivot around the concept of collectives in various forms. This is most applicable if you are a principal or an assistant principal, but if you are an instructional coach, a team leader, a teacher leader, or a PLC facilitator, you, too, are at the forefront of this collaborative force. Your group may manifest as an academic department, a grade-level team, a professional learning community (PLC), or any one of a variety of educator-led initiatives. Regardless of the structure, you are part of a unified effort working toward shared goals.

The intent of this book is to create a sustainable road map for the implementation of effective collaboration with an emphasis on specific leadership and coaching actions. Building on the foundation of *Achievement Teams: How a Better Approach to PLCs Can Improve Student Outcomes and Collective Efficacy* (Ventura & Ventura, 2022), this book offers additional teacher and leadership strategies (paired with resources, examples, and field-tested implementation tactics) to amplify instructional impact and academic outcomes. The purpose is to share contemporary strategies for increasing student achievement through rigorous collaborative dialogue.

Why is this chapter important? There are many indicators of successful school and district leadership. Understanding those indicators and then including them in your overall leadership profile is important, as the leadership practices described in this chapter are directly linked to enhancing student outcomes.

How can it improve your personal leadership profile? Leaders understand that self-reflection and an evaluation of the impact they have is a prerequisite of effective leadership.

The Three Pillars of a Robust Collective

There are three pivotal traits that underscore the essence of all thriving collectives within the educational sphere. These traits—clarity, consistency, and accountability—are often the by-products of visionary leadership that, albeit inadvertently, forges a vision grounded in these foundational principles. This occurs because these leaders operate with a mindset focused on building strong, unified teams. Exceptional leaders grow their leadership capacity through integrity, consistency, and capability, reliably demonstrating these qualities from the beginning to the end of each school day.

The hallmark of effective leadership is the trust and belief that followers vest in their leader. With that in mind, reflect: Do individuals place their trust and belief in you? How do you know? In the following chapters, we will explore these questions and more, aiming to define your understanding of leadership by enriching your practice and enhancing the educational journey for all involved.

We will also delve deeper into the leadership traits that underpin the collective. Leadership within educational settings requires a nuanced approach, one that disregards favoritism, avoids the creation of micro-groups, and is characterized by actions that speak louder than words. Indeed, leadership consistency is about what leaders say and, more important, what they do.

Consider someone you know whose leadership record is undeniably impressive. This person could be a school leader, a bus driver, an administrative support staff member, or someone in any role in between. Reflect on the traits or behaviors that make their leadership skills and presence stand out. Is it their ability to communicate clearly? Their consistent actions? Their equitable treatment of all? All these qualities are crucial, and they underscore the significance of leadership traits that inspire and guide others.

Leadership Clarity

A common sentiment I've encountered in my discussions with teachers captures a significant challenge within leadership. I've heard variations of the following again and again: "If she would just tell us what she wants, we would do it." "We don't know his vision for the school." These frustrations highlight a gap in communication that results in uncertainty and improvisation, as teachers strive to fill in the blanks left by an absence of clear direction. It also underscores the necessity of a leadership profile rooted in clarity and consistency, where both the collective's purpose and the leader's expectations are unequivocally understood.

The collective is predicated on a leadership style that eradicates ambiguity about the group's objectives. Although the adage "we're here for the kids" is a common refrain, a truly effective vision goes beyond such clichés to explicitly define the group's purpose. This clarity of vision is what differentiates mere management from inspirational leadership.

Leadership Consistency

Reflecting on my tenure as a superintendent, the most transformative experiences stemmed from focused and consistent leadership. By focusing on five key initiatives over two years, I was able to sift through countless educational demands, sharpening my leadership focus and enhancing the faculty's ability to utilize student data effectively. This approach was marked by clear communication, established expectations, diligent monitoring, and a commitment to living out our principles, thereby providing constructive feedback and fostering an environment of continuous improvement.

Consistent celebration of milestones is another facet of explicit leadership that merits emphasis. Our collective joy in becoming adept at interpreting data was about more than just student outcomes; it was a celebration of adherence to the process we established and the fidelity of our actions. The distinction between managing and leading is pivotal. Effective leaders are immersed in the practices they advocate for, demonstrating their commitment through active participation in collaborative meetings; engagement with data; and the provision of regular, actionable feedback. By contrast, managers may advocate for PLCs, for example, but remain detached from their execution, choosing to focus on administrative tasks such as budgeting and facilities management without actively supporting instructional improvement.

Some principals and coaches may feel strongly that it's important for leaders to refrain from actively participating in or leading PLCs. I certainly agree that teachers should develop their confidence, expertise, and leadership through strong PLC engagement, but it is essential for leaders to authentically guide and contribute to collaborative teacher teams. This builds credibility, strengthens relationships and trust with teachers, and ensures that PLCs function in pursuit of student achievement and organizational goals.

Instructional leaders distinguish themselves by their relentless pursuit of excellence, always questioning how practices can be improved and modeling the passion and inspiration they wish to see in their teachers. They establish clear focal points for improvement and resist the temptation to chase new initiatives until existing ones are fully integrated and understood.

Leadership Accountability

This leadership journey is akin to navigating a "J curve," where initial accountability measures may dip as new practices are implemented. The challenge lies in persisting through this dip without succumbing to the allure of novel, yet unproven, solutions. True instructional leadership is about steadfastness—a dedication to follow through on all commitments made until tangible improvements are realized—which can foster a culture of inspired, passionate educators who are dedicated to the collective success of their students.

Maximizing Impact with Collective Leadership

To begin the process of evolving into a leader who can lead a collective, you must create a framework that is representative of your leadership vision. As a leader—and someone who has encountered countless leaders throughout your career—you likely have opinions and beliefs about what makes a good leader. So let's explore these beliefs and see if any of them can help strengthen your own leadership skills.

Anticipation Guide

Anticipation guides can be used to activate prior knowledge before information is read or studied. In this activity (see Figure 1.1), you will explore a generalization of upcoming key concepts by indicating whether you agree or disagree with various beliefs about leadership. Later, you will assess your responses to see if your thinking has changed.

Indicators of Effective Teacher Collaboration

Let's begin by examining the foundational elements of effective teacher teams and their methods for improving instructional practice. In *Achievement Teams: How a Better Approach to PLCs Can Improve Student Outcomes and Teacher Efficacy* (Ventura & Ventura, 2022), my co-author and I outlined specific behaviors that are value-added practices when teachers collaborate. Here, I want to take a more focused approach by explaining three profiles of focused collaboration and how to lead these practices.

In successful collaboration, team members must do three things. They must understand that assessment results reflect their instructional effort, follow structured collaboration that features specific protocols, and

FIGURE 1.1
Anticipation Guide

Directions: Respond to each item with Agree or Disagree in the Before column.

Before		Beliefs	After	
Agree	Disagree		Agree	Disagree
		Effective leaders encourage competition with others in the school or district.		
		Leaders can choose the way they want to use their time by prioritizing what needs to be accomplished.		
		Effective leaders adapt their leadership by adjusting different approaches for different situations.		
		Instructional leaders are keenly aware of the instructional practices being incorporated in their buildings.		
		Instructional coaches can increase positive teacher emotions by creating a no-fault reflection process where teachers can learn from mistakes.		
		Instructional coaches should facilitate PLCs and achievement teams.		
		Artificial intelligence can reduce critical thinking and is difficult to integrate with collaboration.		
		Instructional leaders should avoid observing classrooms where they may not have content expertise.		

Were any of these considerations difficult to decipher? Did you struggle to agree or disagree with any of them? Reflect below or with a partner.

_____

_____

_____

_____

appropriate new knowledge about teaching and learning. In order for this to be possible, team members need to have supportive leaders who guide collaborative practices via a shared vision or framework.

Throughout this book, we will examine the role of a leader and how leaders can best support effective team collaboration while still empowering educators to form professional relationships grounded in trust and collective efficacy.

Shaping Your Instructional Leadership Vision

Crafting a vision that precisely articulates your aspirations and strategies for advancing teaching and learning is crucial for any leader responsible for teacher teams or professional learning communities. An effective instructional leadership vision is characterized by

- **Relevance Across the Educational System:** It's essential that your vision resonates with the entire educational community—teachers, staff members, students, and families. How does your vision manifest in the daily practices of each group, and how do these practices differ among stakeholders? Your vision should be dynamic, evolving in response to feedback from your team, personal growth, and data insights.
- **Community-Inspired Focus:** Your school community will look for a vision that mirrors their own ambitions and aspirations. Engage in a collaborative process to craft your vision, actively seeking and incorporating input from your educational community.
- **Forward-Looking Goals:** Define clear, achievable goals for your team in the short and long terms. Vividly imagine the ideal future state of your school, and then guide and inspire everyone toward that vision.
- **An Ability to Turn Vision into Action:** Your vision should not be confined to the pages of a strategic plan or mentioned only during annual orientations. Integrate it into the fabric of your daily school operations. Regularly reference your vision in conversations, meetings, and presentations. Acknowledge and celebrate when actions

and decisions align with your vision, reinforcing its value and guiding principles.

Instructional Leadership Vision Examples

"The role of the instructional leader is a balance between content and organizational leadership" (Kirtman, 2013, p. 8). Effective leaders consider these two factors and develop a vision that is predicated on an ability to create connections within their education community. Furthermore, leaders with a strong sense of efficacy can help others find their vision and optimize their impact.

Examples of strong content leadership include an ability to

- Understand the importance of professional development and invest in a learning environment that seeks to improve practice and increase learning (or that is consistent with the school improvement strategy).
- Set the bar high by pursuing excellence and innovation.
- Lead by example and live the culture you want others to live.
- Increase knowledge and competency—and as a result, normalize challenge and effort.
- Ensure an instructional program that is consistent and delivered with integrity.

Examples of strong organizational leadership include an ability to

- Develop—rather than manage—people.
- Buffer staff from noninstructional issues.
- Champion equity and inclusion.
- Avoid fragmented reform efforts.
- Move from islands of excellence to systematic impact with high levels of collective efficacy and commitment.

In developing and sharing your instructional leadership vision, it's important to engage your team in a manner that welcomes constructive feedback and collaborative refinement. Opening up to feedback, although it may make you feel vulnerable, is invaluable for enhancing your leadership approach. Focus your leadership efforts on effective strategies backed by research and ensure your vision becomes an integral aspect of daily instructional practices.

With a well-defined, collaboratively crafted vision and a commitment to evidence-based leadership practices, you and your team will be well positioned for success. Such an instructional leadership vision will not only drive meaningful improvement in teaching and learning but also build a cohesive, empowered educational community aligned toward shared goals.

"What? So What? Now What?" Critical Reflection Model

This well-established model offers a structured approach to reflection, helping learners move beyond surface-level observations and emotional responses. Although each question—"What?" "So what?" "Now what?"—can yield valuable insights on its own, addressing all three ensures a more comprehensive understanding. This model encourages learners to reflect holistically, integrating facts, emotions, and future actions, and preventing themselves from getting stuck on any one aspect (see Figure 1.2).

FIGURE 1.2
What? So What? Now What? Critical Reflection Model

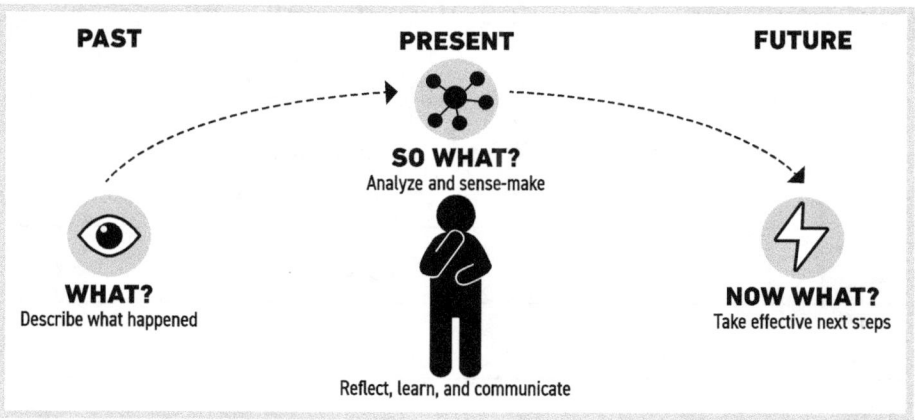

Originally developed by Terry Borton (1970) as a group facilitation method, the framework gained prominence in the 1980s, particularly among clinical healthcare practitioners, as a tool for reflective practice. Today, it remains widely used across various fields, from education to leadership development, helping individuals and teams analyze experiences, derive meaning, and plan actionable steps.

What? In this chapter, we included

1. The meaning and importance of the notion of "the collective" in education.
2. The three pillars of a robust collective (clarity, consistency, and accountability).
3. Ways to maximize impact through collective leadership and self-reflection.
4. Indicators of effective teacher collaboration.
5. Strategies to shape your instructional leadership vision.

So What? What are the implications for this chapter and your leadership framework? What are the implications of the research?

_____

_____

_____

_____

Now What? What will you do differently as a result?

_____

_____

_____

_____

The Purpose of This Book

This book offers research, examples, stories, and strategies to support leaders at all levels as they guide the collectives they serve. Its key focus is about strengthening your role as an instructional leader to lead teacher teams effectively, but it is also about becoming an effective leader beyond the constructs of a team.

My goal is to challenge your assumptions of leadership and redefine your role through insights from relevant research and real-world stories of effective leaders. By the end of this book, you will have both a clear vision of what it means to cultivate a collective mindset and practical tools you can use to lead your own collective—whatever form it may take—with confidence and purpose.

2

HIGHLY EFFECTIVE INSTRUCTIONAL LEADERSHIP

Leading the collective includes being a strong and visible instructional leader, but what does that mean? There is an abundance of research available regarding instructional leadership, but processing that information can be overwhelming. Being an effective K–12 leader is not merely about occupying a position of management but rather about embodying authentic leadership that inspires and empowers others to reach their full potential. Instructional leadership goes beyond a title; it is a mindset, set of values, and way of engaging with others that fosters a positive and inclusive learning environment.

Currently, it seems as though school systems are not always aligned with the academic demands they face, which has been amplified in the years following the COVID-19 pandemic. Also apparent is the lack of leadership to meet these challenges as it seems leaders are being asked to do things they simply do not know how to do. From establishing a vision of clarity to creating collaborative leadership opportunities, few school systems have been able to successfully grasp these issues with solutions and forward progress.

The Role of an Instructional Leader

The truth is that strong instructional leaders can considerably accelerate student achievement, especially if they can support a clear leadership vision and guide teacher teams and PLCs. Effective instructional leadership depends less on programs and more on professional practice rooted in a clear vision. As Michael Fullan (2008) said, "Leaders have to provide direction, create the conditions for effective peer interaction, and intervene along the way when things are not working as well as they could" (p. 49). Today's principals are expected to break down academic, social, and economic barriers to create ideal conditions for learning. However, before tackling such important and, oftentimes, daunting work, principals must create and share their leadership vision in a way that inspires positive action. This vision, when thoughtfully constructed and recalibrated, serves as the guiding light for teams in pursuit of students' academic growth.

With that in mind, let's focus on what makes a strong leadership vision, how to create your vision, and how to get and keep people on board with that vision. Throughout this chapter, we will delve into the data and research that unequivocally demonstrate the positive impact of instructional leadership on student achievement and educator effectiveness to uncover the key characteristics that define collaborative leaders and gain practical guidance on how to cultivate those characteristics.

Why is this chapter important? Leaders explore several key elements that contribute to instructional leadership success, such as vision, indicators for effective collaboration, and the far-reaching role of a leader in student outcomes.

How can it improve your personal leadership profile? Combining and organizing these elements in a cohesive and strategic manner assists school leaders in determining strengths and opportunities for improving their leadership responsibilities, thereby setting a course of action to positively influence student achievement.

The Instructional Leader's Mindset

Instructional leaders are accountable for their contributions to student learning. Their role is to guide teams to understand the purpose of collaboration and how it can improve instruction and achievement. Leaders must model reflective practices to ensure teachers engage in data-informed decision making and adjust instruction based on students' needs. By promoting a shared vision among educators, building trust within teams, and creating a culture of continuous improvement, instructional leaders become the driving force behind the school's success. Beyond facilitating collaboration and providing timely feedback, they empower teachers to take on challenges and celebrate successes.

The truth is that even though the path to academic success for all students may be full of obstacles, it is also paved with opportunities for transformation and growth under skillful instructional leadership.

Think Like a Leader!

Take a moment to reflect on the following prompts and your instructional leadership practice.

1. How do teachers encourage active participation in their classrooms?
2. What roles should students assume in a learner-centered classroom?
3. How do leaders encourage and promote collaboration among students and teachers?
4. How do leaders encourage teachers to reflect on their learning experiences?

Can you identify examples where you were a strong instructional leader? Any examples where you may have contributed more to student learning?

_____

_____

_____

_____

Instructional Leadership in Action: Edison School District

Between 2007 and 2008, the Edison School District in California underwent a profound transformation under the guidance of strong instructional leadership. As superintendent during this pivotal period, I spearheaded efforts that resulted in elevated proficiency levels for students across all demographics. Initially, a disparity in academic performance was evident. Hispanic students, English language learners (ELLs), and economically disadvantaged students lagged behind their white counterparts, according to the Academic Performance Index (API). This situation was further compounded by the threat of state intervention due to the district's poor performance metrics, casting a shadow over morale.

As a newly appointed superintendent, my primary aim was to enhance the API scores through targeted teacher interventions. Together with my leadership team, we identified and implemented four key initiatives poised to make the most significant impact on student achievement:

1. Evidenced-based decision making
2. Prioritized learning targets
3. Assessment literacy and formative assessment
4. Achievement Teams

In my capacity as the district leader, I committed myself to be a learner and a visible figure in the educational process. I ensured that educators were afforded the necessary time and space to dedicate to these initiatives, repurposing a large auditorium within the district for this cause. My engagement extended to participating in sessions led by external consultants in addition to internal collaboration time. I firmly believed in the transformative power of leadership visibility in fostering initiative success; hence, I dedicated my days to working with teachers and reserved administrative tasks for after-school hours.

I was actively involved in the creation of our initial common formative assessments and participated in Achievement Team meetings, where discussions centered on student data and the corresponding actions by adults. My role also entailed celebrating successes with educators and offering constructive feedback for continuous improvement throughout this journey.

The outcomes of these focused efforts were nothing short of remarkable. In less than two years, we successfully elevated our API score from 660 (in 2008) to 705 (in 2009), effectively narrowing the achievement gap between white students and all other student populations. More important, this period marked a significant shift in teacher mindset, fostering a strong sense of collective efficacy that set the stage for sustained districtwide growth and development.

Five Dimensions of Effective School Leadership

In their seminal work, Viviane Robinson and her team uncovered a series of leadership practices that are directly linked to enhancing student outcomes (Robinson et al., 2008). By meticulously associating each practice with an effect size, they provided a quantitative measure of its impact, thereby allowing for a deeper understanding of its significance. The concept of effect size serves as a robust tool for quantifying the differences among groups, offering a clear perspective on the efficacy of various leadership actions. Furthermore, the utilization of meta-analysis in that study enables a comprehensive synthesis of diverse research findings into a unified effect size, focusing on the relationship between leadership actions—whether at the district or principal level—and student achievement.

The study delineates five key practices, or what I would consider leadership outcomes:

1. **Establishing Goals and Expectations:** Highlighting the paramount importance of setting clear, challenging—yet attainable—goals, this practice underscores the role of goal setting in motivating staff and aligning their efforts with organizational objectives. The emphasis on feedback mechanisms further ensures that these goals foster an environment conducive to heightened student achievement.

2. **Ensuring an Orderly and Supportive Environment:** This principle emphasizes the critical role of leadership in creating a learning atmosphere that minimizes disruptions and promotes safety and support. By prioritizing consistent discipline and a nurturing school community, leaders significantly enhance the focus on academic and social objectives.
3. **Planning, Coordinating, and Evaluating Teaching and the Curriculum:** This practice accentuates the difference in leadership approaches between high- and low-performing schools. It advocates for a collaborative ethos among school leaders and staff, aiming to refine and elevate the quality of teaching and learning. The active involvement of leaders in curricular coordination and the fostering of collegial dialogue on instructional matters are identified as key drivers of success.
4. **Promoting and Participating in Teacher Learning and Development:** Far from being mere patrons of professional development, leaders are encouraged to actively engage in learning alongside their staff. This approach not only amplifies their influence on instructional practices but also enhances their credibility and respect among colleagues.
5. **Resourcing Strategically:** Contrary to the notion that successful leadership hinges on acquiring additional funding, this practice stresses the strategic alignment of resources with pivotal educational goals. By focusing efforts and resources on high-impact strategies and initiatives, leaders can achieve a significant improvement in student achievement outcomes.

These practices, grounded in rigorous research, offer a blueprint for school leaders aiming to foster an environment in which student achievement flourishes. It is a call to action for strategic, intentional leadership that is acutely focused on the core mission of educational excellence.

For professional learning communities or teams within schools, these key factors underscore the importance of collaborative leadership, shared goals, and a unified approach to teaching and learning. Embedding these practices within the fabric of PLCs can significantly enhance their effectiveness, fostering an environment in which continuous improvement is not just encouraged but actively pursued. The collective application of these leadership practices within PLCs can serve as a powerful catalyst for elevating student achievement, emphasizing the critical role of strategic leadership in shaping educational outcomes.

Often, people see the activity in Figure 2.1 and feel the primary indicator of student achievement is either establishing goals and expectations or planning, coordinating, and evaluating teaching and the curriculum. This is because principals don't usually see themselves as learning with teachers; instead, they see their role as the one managing the process. If leaders don't

FIGURE 2.1
Ranking the Five Leadership Dimensions

How would you rank the importance of the five leadership dimensions when it comes to the impact each can have on teaching and learning? Rank the importance of each dimension using your own expertise and understanding, with 1 being the most important when it comes to teaching and learning and 5 being the least important. Then see how your rankings measured up!

Leadership Actions	Actual Ranking	Effect Size	Impact
Ensuring an orderly and supportive environment	5	0.27	Medium Exceeding 62% of schools not receiving that treatment
Resourcing strategically	4	0.31	Medium Exceeding 64% of schools not receiving that treatment
Establishing goals and expectations	3	0.42	Medium Exceeding 67% of schools not receiving that treatment
Planning, coordinating, and evaluating teaching and the curriculum	2	0.42	Medium Exceeding 67% of schools not receiving that treatment
Promoting and participating in teacher learning and development	1	0.84	Large Exceeding 82% of schools not receiving that treatment

Note: Cohen (1988) defined effect sizes as "small, $d = 0.2$," "medium, $d = 0.5$," and "large, $d = 0.8$" and stated, "There is a certain risk inherent in offering conventional operational definitions for those terms for use in power analysis in as diverse a field of inquiry as behavioral science" (p. 25).

see themselves as learners, then it is necessary to have a shift in understanding so they re-evaluate their role in professional learning. The key thing to remember is that all five dimensions are powerful and should be part of a comprehensive leadership vision, but the ones with the greatest impact are ironically the ones most often overlooked. The impact of a 0.84 effect size can be associated with two to three years of growth or progress in one instructional year.

The purpose of ranking these actions isn't to disregard any of them—as they all have value—but to truly understand the importance of leaders who are active participants in professional learning. Resourcing strategically has a 0.31 effect size, but don't diminish its value. It's considered medium growth and has a strong impact on student outcomes. Robinson and colleagues' research merely uncovered the idea that leaders who do what they ask others to do have a huge and immediate impact on learning.

By prioritizing these five core areas in your role as a leader, and by clearly communicating these priorities to your team, you position yourself and your school for a year marked by focused growth and achievement. Take some time to assess the impact of your current leadership. Then contemplate mechanisms through which you can seek accountability from others for the action plans you've delineated, integrating these into your broader leadership development strategy for the year. This approach not only promises a pathway to personal and professional growth but also serves as a foundation for fostering a culture of continuous improvement within your educational community—specifically among the teacher teams and PLCs you lead.

Assess Your Leadership Impact

I invite you to embark on a reflective journey regarding your leadership prowess across Robinson and colleagues' (2008) five dimensions. Utilize a 1–5 scale to gauge where your leadership stands presently in each practice, with 1 indicating a pressing need for enhancement and 5 representing exemplary leadership that others could learn from.

1: Urgently requires enhancement

2: Stands to gain from further development

3: Competent and effective

4: Highly competent and effective

5: Exemplary; a benchmark for others

Take a moment to consider: What is one tangible step you could take within the coming week to advance in each of these areas?

_____

_____

_____

_____

Leadership Framework to Improve School Outcomes

Now that you have a vision for the elements needed to be an effective leader, it is essential to establish organizational structures that enable collaborative protocols to thrive. Although people—teachers, leaders, and staff—are the driving force behind school success, sustainable outcomes depend on structures that foster consistent collaboration and accountability. Without these systems, even the most committed individuals may struggle to maintain momentum, leading to fragmented efforts that do not fully benefit students.

The leadership framework presented in Figure 2.2 highlights the interplay between the people-centered practices and organizational structures necessary to support teaching and learning. On the left side of the framework, the focus is on the interactions between leaders and teachers—where practices such as feedback, coaching, and instructional guidance occur. On the right side, the framework identifies the structural elements needed at the organizational level, such as time for collaboration, shared goals, and data systems that support continuous improvement. When instructional leadership practices align with these structures, schools can achieve sustained academic growth and measurable improvements in student outcomes.

FIGURE 2.2
Leadership Framework to Improve School Outcomes

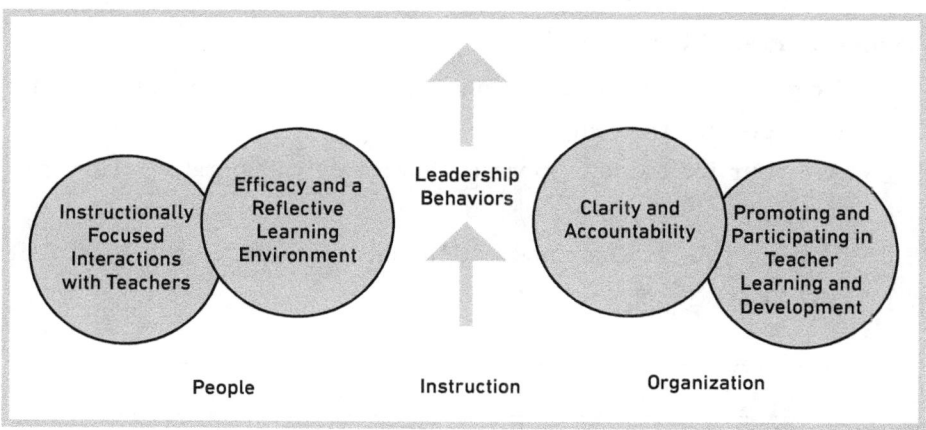

Instructionally Focused Interactions with Teachers

As school leadership evolves, so do interactions with teachers. A majority of these interactions should concentrate on practices that can considerably accelerate student achievement and progress. It is easy to get side-tracked with nonacademic conversations, and there really is no way to avoid this. However, instructional leaders should be keenly aware of the instructional practices that are being incorporated in their buildings. Moreover, effective leaders have learned how to shift conversations focused on individual people to be conversations focused on instructional practices.

This can be modeled in a teacher team or PLC meeting where leaders talk about instruction, specific strategies teachers are using, and the results of those practices. These conversations should be nonjudgmental and an active facilitator in helping teachers choose the best instructional approach—and learn why some approaches work better in various situations. The following activity will help you reflect on people-centered practices and organizational structures.

Assess Your Leadership Framework
The push and pull between supporting people and upholding structures is a delicate dance leaders manage every day. Reflect on how well you

balance people-centered practices with organizational structures to drive student outcomes. Use the following prompts to guide your thinking.

People-Centered Practices
- How often do your conversations with teachers focus on instructional strategies and their impact?
- Are your interactions more evaluative or collaborative? How can you tell?
- How do you refocus conversations on instruction when they drift off topic?

_____

_____

_____

_____

Organizational Structures
- Do you have systems (e.g., PLCs, data protocols) that support meaningful collaboration?
- Are these structures aligned with your instructional goals?
- How do you track whether these structures improve teaching and learning?

_____

_____

_____

_____

Next Steps
Identify one area—either a people-centered practice or an organizational structure—to improve. Write a concrete action you'll take this week to strengthen your leadership framework.

_____

_____

Efficacy and a Reflective Learning Environment

"Critically reflective teachers learn from the past but live in the present with an eye to the future" (Brookfield, 1995, p. 265). Reflective teaching is a practice that helps teachers gain critical understanding of how students learn and the relationship between learning and instructional practice. The Cambridge International Education Teaching and Learning Team (2019) highlights several such practices. The power of reflective teaching normalizes what most educators do intrinsically—becoming acutely aware of their knowledge by "examining assumptions of everyday practice . . . [and] critically evaluating their own responses to practice situations" (Finlay, 2008, p. 1). Many times, self-reflection can remind teachers to energize their ability to affect student learning. Through a series of reflective scenarios, self-reflection is a metacognitive exercise that improves skill acquisition while challenging current thinking and practice.

In 1988, Graham Gibbs introduced the Gibbs Reflective Cycle, which includes the six stages shown in Figure 2.3. Although this cycle was not developed exclusively for teachers, you can see how the cycle adapts to education:

- Description of the experience.
- Feelings and thoughts about the experience.
- Evaluation of the experience, both good and bad.
- Analysis to make sense of the situation.
- Conclusion about what you learned and could have done differently.
- Action plan for how you would deal with similar situations in the future, or general changes you might find appropriate.

Leaders should reinforce the practice of reflection not only for teachers but also for themselves. Remember, instructionally effective schools share a common thread: the leaders in these schools were seen doing what they required others to do. Encourage and model reflective thinking in teacher team and PLC conversations, and provide time for educators to reflect on teaching and learning on a regular basis.

FIGURE 2.3
Gibbs Reflective Cycle

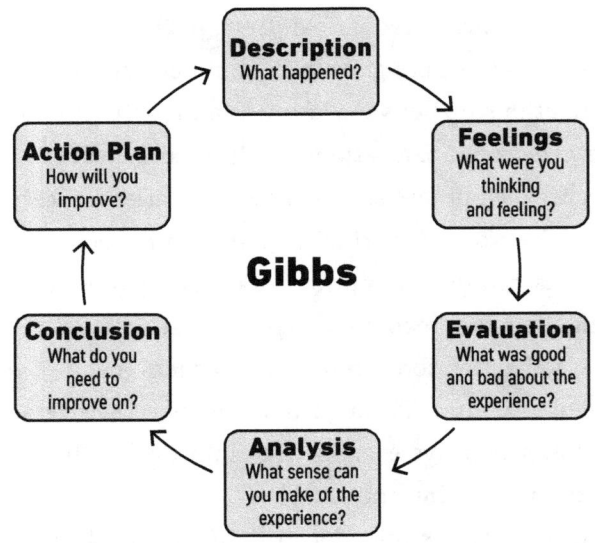

Source: From *Learning by Doing*, by G. Gibbs, 1988. Oxford Centre for Staff and Learning Development. This book is licensed under the CC BY-NC 3.0 license.

Clarity and Accountability

Changing systems of clarity and accountability requires a considerable degree of focus. In fact, major schoolwide initiatives often fail because of a lack of clarity about the meaning, purpose, and expectations of instructional and operational practices. To that end, it's beneficial to create clear expectations for all teachers:

- Communicate on a regular and consistent basis with parents, highlighting their child's progress, attendance, and other important factors that contribute to a successful school experience.
- Actively engage in professional development as a means to work toward professional goals.
- Use collaboration to improve practice and pedagogy that transfers to higher levels of student success.

Without clearly delineated expectations, we risk fostering a culture of confusion with an emphasis on inconsistent implementation and practices. I recognize that the term *accountability* frequently evokes thoughts of test scores and various forms of evaluation. However, in this scenario, accountability signifies a mutual responsibility among individuals. It starts with acknowledging each person's unique contributions, followed by cultivating a dynamic and enthusiastic community of educators who grasp the significance of their united efforts. Lacking this sense of shared responsibility, it becomes challenging for teaching teams to achieve their objectives. Therefore, ensure that everything you expect and ask of educators is clear and transparent. Check in often to see if there is a lack of clarity. Remind teachers often why they are engaging in teacher teams and what you want them to accomplish in these models.

Professional development involves more than principals arranging for staff to learn. One of the most effective leadership traits is when principals enthusiastically participate in learning with others. A leader has a much better opportunity of acquiring instructional impact when they possess the knowledge, skills, and principles they would like others to achieve. Ultimately, when leaders actively engage and learn with others, they tend to earn greater respect from their team.

Track, Monitor, and Adjust Initiative Implementation

Strong instructional leadership requires building-level leaders to track and monitor current levels of initiative implementation. This is possible, but there is one caveat to keep in mind: principals cannot track everything and if they attempt to, there would be no time to improve initiatives. Therefore, the best way to monitor initiatives is to narrow the focus by prioritizing those actions that are worth monitoring and tracking.

Once leaders decide what major tasks to monitor, they can ensure deep, steadfast execution of those initiatives that require monitoring and feedback tools to solidify schoolwide or districtwide efforts. This means focusing on the outcomes of initiatives, such as teacher teams or PLCs, and optimizing or adjusting as needed.

This framework guides the actions that teachers and leaders take to ensure that student outcomes are at the forefront of their instructional practices, coaching behaviors, and leadership practices.

"What? So What? Now What?" Critical Reflection Model

What? In this chapter, we included four key points to define aspects of instructional leadership and its role in collaborative teams:

1. The necessary role of an instructional leader.
2. Essential mindsets of effective instructional leaders.
3. Five dimensions of effective school leadership.
4. Leadership framework to improve school outcomes.

Each key point gives the reader an opportunity to reflect and compare their present leadership profile to the four listed here. There is no single leadership profile that can be applied to every leadership scenario. In short, there is no "one size fits all." However, skilled leaders know how to navigate different leadership traits for different situations.

So What? Based on the research shared, what are the implications for you? How do these key points transfer to practice? When we study effective leadership characteristics, we feel either validated or compelled to make changes depending on if we incorporate some of these traits into our own leadership practices. Now is the time to reflect on how your leadership actions match the profiles of those that make the greatest difference.

_____

_____

_____

_____

Now What? What will you do differently as a result?

_____

_____

_____

_____

I'm fond of the old maxim that continuous improvement is better than delayed perfection, which is particularly relevant here. If you discover that you are missing some critical leadership skills, this is when you decide if there is something different you need to do or add to your leadership vision. As leaders, we must recognize that there are no plateaus. We continually learn, apply, and improve.

3

THE LEADER'S ROLE IN INSTRUCTIONAL STRATEGY SELECTION

Teacher team and PLC collaboration can predictably narrow the achievement gap, especially when the instructional strategies that teachers collectively select are implemented with confidence and competence. In education, we frequently use terms like *evidence-based* or *research-based* instructional strategies. But what does this mean? Research-based instructional strategies are strategies that have been identified, by independent research, to be the most effective at influencing student learning outcomes and student achievement (Prieur, 2022). It is essential for instructional leaders to remain firmly committed to the study, practice, and implementation of proven, high-impact instructional strategies.

The Role of Instructional Strategies in Education

One of the most prominent figures in contemporary education is John Hattie, whose extensive research on evidence-based strategies, *Visible Learning,* has been widely referenced in support of high-impact instruction. Hattie (2012) states that instructional strategies have a singular purpose. The goal is to have students actively engaged in gathering evidence of their learning. Rather than simply completing tasks assigned by teachers, they should take ownership of their progress by monitoring and understanding their learning growth. This involves assessing their own development, taking greater responsibility for their education, and collaborating with peers to reflect on and enhance their learning outcomes.

My own definition is a combination of several straightforward descriptions. Namely, instructional strategies are teacher actions designed to raise student levels of thinking and learning around specific learning targets. They are purposeful methods of instruction that help create vibrant, independent students who can assess their own learning. With Achievement Teams, teachers can improve their practices and classroom environment while putting in place a structured approach to addressing all student needs (Ventura & Ventura, 2022).

Why is this chapter important? Instructional leaders with a strong knowledge of instructional strategies can create additional opportunities for meaningful collaboration, which ultimately promotes student achievement.

How can it improve your personal leadership profile? School leadership improves when leaders are in alignment with effective teaching and learning. By reading academic publications and current books, you can keep a pulse on trends in education and the ever-changing needs of students, as well as the research-based best practices that support student learning and teacher practice. When educational research drives instructional design and implementation within your school, teacher and student performance improves.

Fostering the Use of Instructional Strategies

Throughout this chapter, you will learn specific ways to lead your school or district toward stronger instructional strategy selection, while learning which strategies have a very high probability of significantly accelerating student achievement.

Attempting to capture every strategy with every student learning need would be counterproductive, at least for the purposes of this chapter. However, one of the best ways to understand how to select an instructional strategy is to first determine if the strategy is aligned with the overall need. Administering valid, reliable assessments can absolutely provide strong evidence on how to choose a learning target founded on a data-based learning need. Assessment can drive student achievement and is critical as principals lead their school's PLC journey.

The reality is that many school leaders avoid instructional leadership or coaching because they don't feel as if they possess the content knowledge required to help teachers make instructional decisions. Despite this belief, there does not seem to be significant evidence to support a direct correlation between content expertise and student achievement. For example, studies have found that teachers' knowledge of mathematics and student outcomes actually had a low correlation (e.g., Hattie et al., 2017; Jitendra et al., 2016). Thus, it is possible to demonstrate complete knowledge of your content and still not be a master teacher. What follows are two examples of instructional strategies that instructional leaders might propose to teacher teams and PLCs.

Spaced practice, also known as *distributed practice*, involves spreading learning sessions out over time with breaks in between. This approach divides study time by having students work on various subjects one after the other or engage in other activities between study sessions. By contrast, *massed practice* is a continuous task and usually completed in a single long instructional session, instead of through frequent reviews. Spaced practice, which is presented in smaller chunks over time and includes rest time between intervals, helps students retain information longer. It requires students to recall learning over longer periods of time, which is proven to better solidify concepts for lasting understanding (Rohrer & Pashler, 2007). For example, if students are required to learn new vocabulary, you might use question banks to draw random vocabulary questions so students are not retaking the same quiz every time or returning to earlier vocabulary words throughout a course. To clarify, it is acceptable that they are not doing the same thing repeatedly, but it is spaced out over time and remains continued practice with added progression.

Similarly, *content chunking* is another excellent strategy because it combines smaller chunks of learning with success criteria and provides multiple opportunities for learners to recall information that is delivered in more manageable, bite-size pieces. Spaced practice and content chunking highlight how leaders can use learning strategies without being curriculum experts. This means that the leader doesn't need to be an expert in the content area but an expert in being able to help teachers understand strategies that are significantly proven to accelerate learning. Rather than feeling the need to have content expertise in every academic subject, instructional leaders can confidently lean on high-impact strategies that can be used across various content areas and are not just limited to reading or math.

Leadership to Move from Surface-Level to Deep Learning

Somewhat ironically, the ability to have meaningful conversations about instruction has little to do with whether a leader can teach all subjects. What leaders really need to know is if students are moving beyond instruction focused on low-level recall and memorization. This can be considered foundational learning and is a necessary step in the teaching-learning continuum; however, teachers and leaders need to know how to move students from surface-level to deep learning. Therefore, instructional leaders should recognize the difference between the two and the strategies that accompany them.

Surface-level learning is factual learning, which is a prerequisite for deeper learning. In *Achievement Teams* (Ventura & Ventura, 2022), I encourage the use of learning progressions that contain prerequisite skills and concepts (surface-level learning) that lead to more advanced skills and concepts (deep learning). The former focuses on recall or procedural information, such as explaining, naming, note taking, and restating. The latter is a product of the former, where students can revisit and recall their surface-level knowledge and use it to obtain deeper learning. It requires students to draw on and extend their prior knowledge, such as analyzing similarities and differences, drawing conclusions, and developing logical arguments.

Metacognition represents an example of deep learning, where students become aware of their own thought processes through self-reflection after learning has occurred. When students reflect, they grow more confident and willing to take on new challenges. However, as Hattie (2009) explains, far too many teachers tend to stay at the surface level. In fact, nearly 90 percent of instruction is designed to be at the surface level of learning.

The matrix in Figure 3.1 combines 12 highly effective instructional strategies with the three phases of learning (surface, deep, and transfer) so users can make decisions about optimal learning strategies. After defining *surface, deep,* and *transfer learning,* we dive into the recommended instructional strategies with corresponding skills, engagement examples, and tips to support each level of student learning. Each strategy has suggested student engagement moves that are proven to activate learning. Question stems and prompts that demand various levels of surface, deep, and transfer thinking are also included.

The Three *C*s: Instructional Leaders' Influence on Student Motivation and Engagement

Student engagement and student motivation are influenced by the actions that teachers and leaders take to create learning environments that foster connection. Student motivation is about internal drive, where students demonstrate self-regulation strategies and invest in the effort of learning. They can self-assess their work, analyze their work, and provide internal feedback to determine if their answers are correct. Student engagement is participatory, in theory, where students are actively engaged in classroom learning activities, such as peer tutoring, classroom discussions, and cooperative learning. The challenge is determining if highly motivated students are engaged and if engaged students are motivated to learn.

FIGURE 3.1
Surface, Deep, and Transfer Matrix

Surface Learning: Building Knowledge and Making Connections

Strategy and Skills	Strategy Engagement Examples	Strategy Tips
Outlining: Using an outline at the beginning of the writing process helps learners clarify ideas while demonstrating the student's thinking process. • Arrange • Illustrate • Categorize • Classify	• Graphic organizer (Flipbook page 11) • Timeline of events • Reverse outline	1. Model the strategy during "unit zero" or the beginning of a unit. 2. Cue students when to stop and take notes, then scaffold cues away as students become more self-sufficient. 3. Provide a "notes answer key" so students can check their notes. 4. Digitize outlining and note taking with tools like Creately, Corgi, or Miro.
Note Taking: Recording key information is a powerful cognitive tool that actively engages the brain to retain information while increasing self-efficacy. • Define • Recall facts • Organize • Categorize	• Concept mapping (Flipbook page 6) • Illustrate meanings • Visual images	

Summarizing: Capturing the most important ideas while excluding irrelevant and repetitive information improves memory and comprehension.
• Restate
• Organize information
• Summarize major events
	• GIST (Flipbook page 10)
	• Captioned photo summaries
	• Headline summaries
		1. Give students a limit on how many words they can use in their summary. For example, you could tell them that each word costs $1 and they have a spending limit of $20.
		2. Ask students the following framework questions:
		  a. What are the main ideas?
		  b. What are the crucial details necessary for supporting the main ideas?
		  c. What information is irrelevant or unnecessary?
		3. Round out vocabulary word understanding with a definition, using in a sentence, and drawing a picture or visual representation.

Vocabulary Instruction: Improve comprehension through the use of context clues, defining words in context, sketching words to show meaning, analyzing word parts, and semantic mapping. • Recite • Identify patterns • Interpret • Use context clues	• Card sorts (Flipbook page 5) • Sketching words to show meaning • Analyzing word parts	

(continued)

FIGURE 3.1
Surface, Deep, and Transfer Matrix (continued)

Deep Learning: Making Meaning

Strategy and Skills	Strategy Engagement Examples	Strategy Tips
Metacognition: When students become aware of their own thought process by reflecting after learning has occurred, they are more confident and willing to take on new challenges. • Make observations • Compare • Draw conclusions • Explain	• Exit ticket or journal prompt (Flipbook page 13) • Error analysis (Flipbook page 8) • Self-reported grades (Flipbook page 21)	1. Give students opportunities to share questions and confusion: *What questions do you have? What was most confusing about the material we explored today?* 2. Think aloud and model your thought process by asking and answering the following questions: *What do I know about this topic? Have I done a task like this before? What strategies worked last time? What do I need to do first? How am I doing? What should I do next? Should I try a different strategy? What could I do differently next time?*
Class Discussion: During high-quality formal class discussions, the teacher designs a scenario for students to discuss a specific topic. The teacher becomes the facilitator with prepared, purposeful questions and invites students to speak, ask questions, and justify their thinking. • Interpret • Develop logical arguments • Justify • Cite evidence	• Think-ink-pair-share (Flipbook page 27) • Jigsaw I & II (Flipbook page 12) • Fishbowl	
Concept Mapping: Concept maps, like flowcharts, help learners chunk information based on meaningful connections while allowing them to visualize relationships between different topics. • Compare and contrast • Analyze similarities and differences • Organize • Draw conclusions	• Concept mapping (Flipbook page 6) • Graphic organizers (Flipbook page 11) • Flowchart	1. Create a partially completed map with some concepts and labels missing, and have students fill in the blanks. 2. Model reciprocal teaching for students and ask them to share what they notice. 3. Chart or distribute role cards to clarify student role expectations. Give students time to offer one another affirming and adjusting feedback on fulfilling their roles. 4. Digitize concept mapping with tools like Popplet, MindMeister, and Prezi.
Reciprocal Teaching: Students learn how to ask meaningful questions when they are actively engaged in the learning process through a structured dialogue. • Predict • Summarize • Question • Connect	• Reciprocal teaching (Flipbook page 19) • Send-a-problem (Flipbook page 22) • Student roles for active engagement: summarizer, clarifier, questioner, and predictor	

Transfer Learning: Applying Understanding

Strategy and Skills	Strategy Engagement Examples	Strategy Tips
Identifying Similarities and Differences: Comparing and contrasting strategies, like metaphors and analogies, help learners make connections to prior knowledge and categorize concepts. • Make observations • Connect and relate ideas • Use evidence to justify • Compare and contrast	• Contracts or independent projects (Flipbook page 7) • Debate from a given perspective • Conduct or critique a designed investigation	1. Model peer tutoring to demonstrate characteristics of productive feedback, as well as the differences between directive and nondirective tutoring. 2. List peer tutoring prompts to encourage on-task conversation. 3. Provide students with a peer tutoring graphic organizer to streamline feedback.
Peer Tutoring: When students are paired together, it's a win-win. Both the tutor and the tutee benefit from improved communication, content mastery, and peer relationships. • Explain how • Assess • Synthesize • Apply information from more than one discipline	• Feedback (Flipbook page 9) • Teammates consult (Flipbook page 26) • Teach-write-discuss	
Problem-Solving Teaching: Presenting students with real-world problems to investigate, think critically about, and collaborate to solve allows them to consolidate knowledge with ease. • Make connections • Use evidence to justify • Design and conduct • Produce-present	• Metacognitive inquiry writing (Flipbook page 14) • Practice and challenge by choice (Flipbook page 17) • Project-based learning	1. Provide students with prompts that support them in coaching one another's problem solving. 2. Review rubrics for effective presentations. 3. Allot time daily or weekly for students to share transdisciplinary connections. Post these on a unit bulletin board or other prominent place.
Transforming Conceptual Knowledge: Debates, simulations, and case studies help learners progress from sorting and classifying information to making connections among ideas and, finally, to transferring concepts. • Connect and relate ideas • Applying information from more than one discipline • Self-assess using success criteria • Make generalizations	• RAFT (Flipbook page 18) • Learning menus (Flipbook page 15) • Debates or Socratic seminar • Collaborative note taking • Word splash strategy	

(continued)

FIGURE 3.1
Surface, Deep, and Transfer Matrix (continued)

Question Stems

Surface Learning	Deep Learning	Transfer Learning
Designed to help students gain foundational skills and move them into making connections.	*Designed to help students move from making connections between skills and concepts to raising their level of cognition to probe reasoning and in-depth integration of conceptual knowledge.*	*Designed to raise students' level of cognition from strategic thinking to extending their ability to transfer prior knowledge to new and novel situations.*
• Can you recall ____? • What is the formula for ____? • How can you recognize ____? • What approach/tools would you use to ____? • How would you apply what you learned to develop ____? • How are ____ alike/different? • What questions would you ask in an interview/survey about ____? • How can you find the meaning of ____? • Can you explain how ____ affected ____? • How would you apply what you learned to develop ____? • How would you compare/contrast ____? • How would you classify ____? • How could you show your understanding of ____? • Can you identify ____? • What examples/nonexamples can you find to show ____? • How would you organize ____ to show ____?	• How or why would you summarize ____? • What examples/nonexamples can you find to ____? • How would you organize ____ to show ____? • How could you show your understanding of ____? • What approach/tools would you use to ____? • How would you apply what you learned to develop ____? • Explain and apply abstract terms and concepts to real-world situations. • What is your prediction and why? • How would you organize these facts/observations? • If you changed these elements ____, what would/might happen? • What facts are relevant to show ____? • What questions would you ask in an interview/survey about ____? • What question is being asked in this problem? • How can you prove that your solution or estimate is reasonable?	• Can you construct a model that would change ____? • Can you think of an original way to apply ____? • Write a thesis, drawing conclusions from multiple sources. • Design and conduct an experiment. • Gather information to develop alternative explanations for the results of the experiment. • Write a research paper on a topic. • Apply information from one text to another text to develop a persuasive argument. • What changes would you make to solve or address this major problem or issue? • How would you improve upon this invention or innovation? • Can you propose an alternative solution to ____? • In what way would you design or redesign ____? Why? • What evidence would you cite to defend the actions of ____? • How would you prioritize criteria for making this decision? Why?

Visit here for more information, strategy templates, and question stems: https://www.steveventura.com/wp-content/uploads/2025/01/ACS-Rigor-Matrix-1.pdf

In addition, engagement can be either emotional or cognitive—or it can include both influences. In fact, it's best if the two happen simultaneously. Emotional engagement is when students feel a sense of belonging and enjoyment toward learning, and cognitive engagement is when students see value in investing in learning that is challenging (Pilotti et al., 2017).

In *Confronting the Crisis of Engagement: Creating Focus and Resilience for Students, Staff, and Communities,* Reeves and colleagues (2022) write that engagement involves effective communication and relationships between student and teacher. In addition to communication, there are three *C*s that improve student engagement: conditions, collaboration, and challenge.

You need to set the **conditions** for a high level of emotional safety. Namely, you want to cultivate a culture in which mistakes are accepted, errors aren't permanent, and students get multiple opportunities to demonstrate proficiency.

Students also need to know that **collaboration** and learning from others is essential. Effective collaboration requires a thoughtfully structured environment, but make no mistake—collaboration and cooperative learning have a very high effect, especially when cooperative learning permits small groups of learners working together to accomplish a shared goal. This allows students at different ability levels to use their strengths to maximize learning for themselves and the larger group. Learners who work together using higher-order thinking skills can solve complex problems. Studies have shown that when implemented correctly, cooperative learning leads to improved student attendance, behavior, achievement, and self-confidence in the classroom.

Every student's learning journey must also include **challenge.** Without challenge, learning becomes repetitive, causing students to lose curiosity while denying them the opportunity to overcome difficulties. Challenge in learning helps students develop a sense of effort, thus increasing their skill acquisition. Bandura (1989) suggests that introducing challenges is key to developing students' skills and self-confidence. When tasks are too easy, success doesn't significantly boost one's sense of ability, but overcoming a moderate degree of challenge leads to more rewarding and motivating achievements. In simple terms, effort builds intelligence.

As instructional leaders, it is advantageous to use the three *Cs* to gauge the level of overall student engagement in a school. The Surface, Deep, and Transfer Matrix in Figure 3.1 can help you toward this end. Later in this chapter, I'll discuss the relationship between the matrix and the Instructional Strategy Flipbook and how to introduce teachers to both tools.

Achievement Teams and Instructional Leadership

Achievement Teams are not only about maintaining existing knowledge but also about the collaborative effort of appropriating new knowledge about teaching and learning. This collaborative component of Achievement Teams, when members are united in their mission and committed to structured protocols while challenging current thinking and practice, fosters a sense of belonging and support among educators. To ensure deep understanding of the content in this chapter, let's engage in a high-level review of the Achievement Teams protocol (Figure 3.2).

The Achievement Teams framework is a four-step structured protocol that prioritizes student achievement and teacher growth. In Step 1, teams collect, organize, and chart the quantitative data to build a strong foundation for the remaining three steps. In Step 2, teams craft SMART goals to create a growth target for students between the pre- and post-assessments. SMART goals are **s**pecific, **m**easurable, **a**chievable, **r**elevant, and **t**ime-bound.

In Step 3, teams develop baseline evidence statements, which are summary statements based on results from formative assessment, helping

FIGURE 3.2
Achievement Teams Protocol

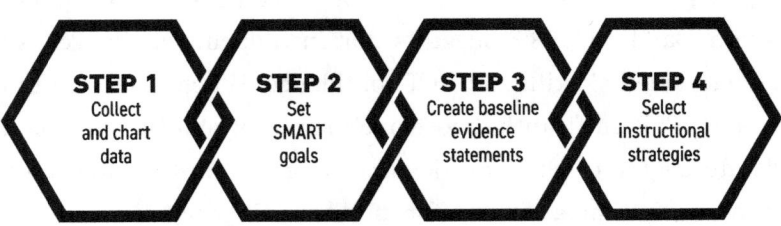

teachers make inferences about student performance levels. Starting with root cause analysis of pre-assessment results, teachers engage in discussions to help reflect on instructional practice.

Finally, in Step 4, teams select high-impact instructional strategies meant to address student needs and advance learning. The strategies are chosen based on the strengths and gaps identified through the pre-assessment and root cause analysis. They are implemented deliberately and practiced with fidelity with the expectation of bridging achievement gaps and developing student strengths.

Five Domains of Instructional Strategies

 The flipbook, created by Michelle Ventura (also found here: www.steveventura.com/wp-content/uploads/2024/08/at-flip-book-web-012223.pdf), includes 25 carefully selected instructional strategies, all chosen for their proven effectiveness in positively affecting student achievement and growth. The inclusion of these strategies in the flipbook is a reassurance to educators about their potential to increase student achievement, instilling a sense of confidence in their effectiveness.

One of my colleagues, Ashley Taplin, thoughtfully designed a play card for the flipbook. This tool was specifically created to help teachers choose instructional strategies based on the learning intention. The play card organizes all instructional strategies into five domains: teacher-led, connect or introduce, collaborative learning, reflect on learning, and build independence (Figure 3.3).

Teacher-led instruction is direct instruction in which the teacher delivers or presents content to the students. Explicit teacher-led instruction, along with success criteria, provides clarity for students. The teacher states the purpose, provides specific instructions, and presents content clearly and directly. Teacher-led instruction is necessary because it helps students understand patterns, organize knowledge, and improve critical thinking skills. In addition, the teacher has the opportunity to control and model the lesson.

FIGURE 3.3
Achievement Teams Instructional Strategy Play Card

Teacher-Led	Connect or Introduce	Collaborative Learning	Reflect on Learning	Build Independence	Focus Questions for Observational Data
Graphic Organizers	Anchor Activities	Jigsaw/Jigsaw II	Error Analysis	Menus	1. What are the assessment results strengths and gaps? 2. What skills and concepts were achieved from the learning target? What still needs to be learned? 3. Who did we teach effectively? Who still needs help? 4. Which strategies were used effectively? Which ones were not?
Scaffolding	Card Sort	Numbered Heads Together	GIST Summarizing Activity	Contracts/Independent Projects	
Study Skills	Concept Mapping	Reciprocal Teaching	Exit Cards/Journal Prompts	Practice and Challenge by Choice	
		Send-a-Problem	Inquiry Writing	Self-Reported Grades	
		Teammates Consult	Feedback	Success Criteria	
		Think-Ink-Pair-Share	RAFT	Tiered Assignments	
			Single-Point Rubric		

Note: Created in partnership with Ashley Taplin and Steve Ventura. Used with permission.

Connecting or introducing students to the lesson is essential. When a teacher can connect with learners, participation will increase, and students become receptive to learning important concepts. Connecting ideas and content also gives students a platform from which to work. Students will be more motivated and invested in learning if they find a connection to what they are about to learn.

Collaborative learning involves groups of students working together to achieve a common goal, complete a task, or solve a problem. This method of instruction emphasizes interaction, shared responsibility, and collective problem-solving. Collaborative learning strategies require students to actively engage with one another, share ideas, and work toward a mutual understanding or outcome. Collaborative learning can increase student engagement by creating a more interactive and dynamic learning environment.

Reflecting on learning after a lesson is a valuable practice that supports deep learning, critical thinking, and personal growth. By incorporating reflection into educational experiences, educators can help learners better understand themselves, the learning process, and the broader context in which they operate. Engagement and memory improve when students are encouraged to reflect on their work. This reflective process allows learners to consider what they have learned, how they learned it, and how it applies to their broader understanding or future learning.

Building independence strategies are designed to develop students' ability to learn, think, and work autonomously. This strategy empowers students to take charge of their learning, make decisions, solve problems, and manage their time. Building independence has many benefits, such as increased student learning outcomes, motivation, and self-confidence. Ultimately, independent learning strategies help develop lifelong learners.

Choosing instructional strategies is a critical part of the Achievement Teams process. As educators, we want to maximize student growth and close learning gaps. Using results from the pre-assessment and taking a deep dive into the strengths and gaps in student learning helps teachers stop using a floodlight to try to cover everything and start using a flashlight to focus on the areas that will help students move forward in the learning process. The

Instructional Strategy Flipbook and play card tool will help teacher teams develop powerful strategies that deepen student learning.

The Instructional Strategy Flipbook

The Instructional Strategy Flipbook features a specific format that accompanies all 25 strategies. First, it briefly describes the strategy, including its purpose and the research behind it. Then the strategy is broken out into four specific considerations:

1. **What's the point of the strategy?** This allows leaders to provide clarity to teacher teams by asking them about and determining the point of using each strategy with students. This is a necessary step, and all the strategies include a list of benefits.
2. **How do I prepare for the strategy?** Here, the strategy starts to transfer to practice through an explanation of how to prepare the strategy for a lesson.
3. **How is the strategy used by students?** An important piece of instructional leadership is to make certain that teacher teams understand not only how students can use the strategy but also how they can progress. For example, many of the strategies listed in the flipbook help students access prior knowledge, see relationships between and among ideas, and reflect on their work, all while self-evaluating their thinking and making corrections.
4. **How is the strategy used by teachers?** This is a critical piece of the flipbook. Teachers need details about *how* they can use a strategy, along with reasons *why* they would use a particular strategy.

One of the ways I introduce this resource is by having teachers select and review a strategy they have never used or are not familiar with. This encourages teacher teams to use new strategies (that have proven to be effective) and allows for thoughtful discussion and learning. Say, for example, a team wants to learn about RAFT (Role, Audience, Format, Topic), which is a strategy that motivates and encourages creative and divergent thinking—and provides a solid check for understanding by inviting students to respond from a perspective other than their own.

1. **What's the point of the strategy?** RAFT allows learners to take the knowledge they gained in one context or situation and use it in a new context or situation to see its relevance and make clear connections.
2. **How do I prepare for the strategy?**
    a. Select content that students need to process, review, and understand.
    b. Determine the possible roles that are appropriate for students to assume, along with possible formats and audiences. Be sure to consider levels of complexity while creating the tasks to ensure rigor and alignment with the measurement's priority standard or learning target.
    c. Create and distribute a table outlining the components of the RAFT.
    d. Assign students one of the four roles, audiences, formats, and topics across the horizontal cells of the table.
    e. Consider readiness, interest, and style in assigning students, or allow choice if levels of challenge are carefully aligned.
3. **How is the strategy used by students?** RAFT is a writing strategy that helps students understand their role as writers, the audience they will address, the varied formats for writing, and the assigned topic.
4. **How is the strategy used by teachers?** RAFT helps students understand their role as writers from multiple perspectives and can be used in all subject areas.

Let's take a look at one more example. Practice and Challenge by Choice empowers students to make choices that demonstrate their learning, motivates students to become self-directed learners, enhances the development of critical thinking skills, and prepares students for real-world experiences. There is a strong link between levels of student concentration, persistence, and engagement in school and achievement outcomes (as demonstrated by the meta-analysis here: www.visiblelearningmetax.com/influences/view/concentration-persistence-engagement). Let's apply the four considerations to unpack this strategy.

1. **What's the point of the strategy?** Providing choice for students allows them the opportunity to demonstrate their understanding of a topic. Teacher-organized stations allow students to review content areas that they need to practice, extend their learning through tackling real-world problems, and collaborate with peers to enhance their skills in a particular content area. Students choose an activity or station based on their self-assessment of a concept or on a teacher's assessment of their need.
2. **How do I prepare for the strategy?**
    a. Structure a formative assessment (often given the day before) on key concepts.
    b. Direct students to review results and select from a menu of activities to determine how to spend time during the review period. Provide self-checks and answer keys with various activities.
    c. Have students self-evaluate after each activity, noting what they know and what they need to study.
    d. Have an anchor activity students can begin if they finish early.
3. **How is the strategy used by students?** Practice and Challenge by Choice allows students to choose differentiated problems they think will benefit them on future assessments and tackle challenging problems to extend their learning.
4. **How is the strategy used by teachers?** Practice and Challenge by Choice allows teachers to provide remediations for students struggling with a topic and challenge stations for students who are ready to move on to deep and transfer learning.

What are the advantages of having teachers and leaders become familiar with the five instructional domains? For starters, it helps create a common academic language throughout the school or district that can be applied to collaborative meetings and teacher planning time. In addition, leaders can increase their own knowledge of high-yield instructional strategies that foster student engagement and meaningful progress. Finally, think of the positive conversations that can be extended using this resource.

Such conversations might sound like this:

- How do you typically select instructional strategies? What evidence do you use to select these strategies?
- Tell me about the instructional strategies you use that are most effective? Least effective?
- What is one area of instruction you feel you can improve? How can I support you in this area?
- Can you share a time where you introduced a strategy to your students and it was not as successful as you had anticipated? What happened?

After this conversation, both the teacher and leader can refer to the Instructional Strategy Flipbook *together*, making connections to the five domains and relevant strategies. As a leader, it is important to demonstrate that you are willing to learn with teachers. Remember, leaders don't need to have all the answers, but they do need to know how to ask the right questions.

Combining the Surface, Deep, and Transfer Matrix with the Instructional Strategy Flipbook

The Surface, Deep, and Transfer Matrix and Instructional Strategy Flipbook are designed to work together so collaborative teams not only have access to highly effective instructional strategies but also gain a working knowledge of how to implement the three phases of learning (Stern et al., 2021). These phases consist of surface (acquiring knowledge of single concepts), deep (connecting concepts in relationship), and transfer (applying to new situations) learning.

An understanding of the three phases of learning adds tremendous value as teams discuss, research, and apply learning strategies. It's critical to remember the type of instruction students currently receive. Hattie (2015) posits that 90 percent of classroom instruction is surface learning, so how can educators better select strategies that align with deep and transfer learning? How do teachers currently select instructional strategies as they examine and analyze assessment results?

"Transfer learning [is] the point at which students take their consolidated knowledge and skills and apply what they know to new scenarios and different contexts. It is also a time when students are able to think metacognitively, reflecting on their own learning and understanding" (Hattie et al.,

2017, p. 32). In short, all transfer is achieved by comparing what we already understand to a new situation. Therefore, transfer learning encourages students to apply their knowledge by constructing understanding through metacognition and performance-based tasks rather than by simply focusing on getting the correct answers.

The Surface, Deep, and Transfer Matrix is organized according to the three learning phases, and there are four high-leverage instructional strategies included for each phase.

Surface Learning Instructional Strategies
1. **Outlining:** Using an outline at the beginning of the writing process helps learners clarify ideas while demonstrating their thinking process.
2. **Note Taking:** Recording key information is a powerful cognitive tool that actively engages the brain to retain information while increasing self-efficacy.
3. **Summarizing:** Capturing the most important ideas while excluding irrelevant and repetitive information improves memory and comprehension.
4. **Vocabulary Instruction:** Improve comprehension through the use of context clues, defining words in context, sketching words to show meaning, analyzing word parts, and semantic mapping.

Deep Learning Instructional Strategies
1. **Metacognition:** When students become aware of their own thought processes by reflecting after learning has occurred, they become more confident and willing to take on new challenges.
2. **Class Discussion:** During high-quality formal class discussions, the teacher designs a scenario for students to discuss a specific topic. The teacher becomes the facilitator with prepared, purposeful questions and invites students to speak, ask questions, and justify their thinking.
3. **Concept Mapping (Thinking Maps):** Concept maps, like flowcharts, help learners chunk information based on meaningful connections while allowing them to visualize relationships between different topics.

4. **Reciprocal Teaching:** Students learn how to ask meaningful questions when they are actively engaged in the learning process through a structured dialogue.

Transfer Learning Instructional Strategies
1. **Identifying Similarities and Differences:** Compare and contrast strategies, such as metaphors and analogies, help learners make connections to prior knowledge and categorize concepts.
2. **Peer Tutoring:** When students are paired together, it's a win-win. Both the tutor and tutee benefit from improved communication, content mastery, and peer relationships.
3. **Problem-Solving Teaching:** Presenting students with real-world problems to investigate, think critically about, and collaborate to solve allows them to consolidate knowledge with ease.
4. **Transforming Conceptual Knowledge:** Debates, simulations, and case studies help learners progress from sorting and classifying information to making connections between ideas and, finally, to transferring concepts.

Application

Let's assume you are looking to suggest an instructional strategy based on deep learning, which is a product of surface learning. It occurs when students can revisit and recall surface-level knowledge and use it to obtain deeper learning. In other words, deep learning connects surface learning to help students progress to higher levels of achievement. Deep learning can be considered an extension of students' prior knowledge.

Class discussion is considered a deep learning instructional strategy. The Surface, Deep, and Transfer Matrix suggests strategies to foster better classroom discussions by referencing page numbers in the Instructional Strategy Flipbook. Under the heading "Activate Student Engagement," there is a parenthetical using this format: (Flipbook page p. 27). This simply means that to encourage better classroom discussion, a teacher should reference page 27 of the Instructional Strategy Flipbook. On page 27, the instructional strategy is think-pair-share.

The Surface, Deep, and Transfer Matrix is designed to help team members select strategies that are aligned with the correct level of rigor or cognitive demand. When the matrix and flipbook are combined, teachers can raise students' levels of thinking and learning around specific learning targets. The strategies are purposeful methods of instruction that help create vibrant, independent students who can assess their own learning.

Find Someone Activity

One of the ways teachers can become familiar with the flipbook is to complete the graphic organizer in Figure 3.4. This can be done during a staff meeting, professional development time, or teacher planning time. The goal is for teachers to find someone who can help fill in one or more of the topics listed in each square. Consequently, teachers could speak to up to nine different colleagues in order to complete all nine squares. Of course, before the activity starts, there can be an agreement on how many squares should be completed. However, I have found that doing all nine makes for a better activity.

Once teachers complete all or some of the graphic organizer, you can reveal the completed form shown in Figure 3.5, which allows them to compare their answers to the exemplars. For example, if you are seeking a strategy that encourages students to articulate the next learning steps (number 5), then teachers can turn to page 24 of the Instructional Strategy Flipbook, which provides detailed information on how to accomplish this task with students.

FIGURE 3.4
Find Someone Activity Graphic Organizer

Find someone who can tell you . . .

1. One way to help students be self-reliant and self-regulate their learning.	2. A way to promote metacognition (i.e., thinking about your thinking).	3. An assessment that yields immediate data.
4. A note-taking and summarizing skill.	5. A way for students to articulate their next learning steps.	6. A strategy that stresses resiliency and inspires students to challenge themselves.
7. A strategy for students to set their own goals.	8. A suggestion to help motivate learners.	9. A strategy that helps students see errors as opportunities and be comfortable saying they don't know and/or need help.

FIGURE 3.5
Completed Find Someone Activity Graphic Organizer

Find someone who can tell you . . .

1. One way to help students be self-reliant and self-regulate their learning. **Learning Menus** are differentiated learning forms that give students a choice of learning activities through a menu format. Learning Menus or choice boards can be created in a variety of styles and mediums, whether online or on paper. Flipbook page 15	2. A way to promote metacognition (i.e., thinking about your thinking). **Inquiry Writing** is a reflective strategy to help students process content. Inquiry Writing incorporates metacognition (i.e., planning how to approach a learning task, evaluating progress, and monitoring comprehension). Flipbook page 14	3. An assessment that yields immediate data. **Exit Tickets/Journal Prompts** are tools for gathering information on student readiness levels, interests, or learning profiles, using predetermined prompts related to the content or activity that focuses on instruction. These prompts can be collected before, during, or after an instructional period. Flipbook page 13
4. A note-taking and summarizing skill. **GIST** (Generating Interactions between Schemata and Texts) is a summarization procedure that helps students digest complex texts by requiring contextual word learning. This strategy provides all students with the opportunity to understand and gain access to rigorous and complex texts deeply. Flipbook page 10	5. A way for students to articulate their next learning steps. **Success Criteria** identifies the details needed to achieve the learning intention. Success Criteria is something students will say, do, make, or write to indicate they are moving toward the learning intention. Flipbook page 24	6. A strategy that stresses resiliency and inspires students to challenge themselves. **Practice and Challenge by Choice** empowers students to make choices to demonstrate their learning, motivates them to become self-directed learners while developing critical thinking skills, and prepares them for real-world experiences. Flipbook page 17
7. A strategy for students to set their own goals. **Self-Reported Grades** refers to a practice by which students assess their performance on a given objective or assessment. There is a strong relationship between students' predicted performance and their actual level of achievement. Flipbook page 21	8. A suggestion to help motivate learners. **RAFT** (Role, Audience, Format, Topic) is a strategy that motivates and encourages creative and divergent thinking. It provides a solid check for understanding by inviting students to respond from a perspective other than their own. Flipbook page 18	9. A strategy that helps students see errors as opportunities and be comfortable saying they don't know and/or need help. **Numbered Heads Together** provides a structure for students to collectively make and learn from errors. Their conversations can assist in understanding the goals, learning intentions, and success criteria. Flipbook page 16

"What? So What? Now What?" Critical Reflection Model

What? In this chapter, we included five components related to concretely defining an effective instructional leader's role within instructional strategy:

1. Fostering the use of instructional strategies.
2. Instructional leadership to move from surface to deep learning and the Surface, Deep, and Transfer Matrix.
3. Instructional leaders' influence on student motivation and engagement through use of the three Cs (conditions, collaboration, and challenge).
4. Achievement Teams and instructional leadership.
5. Five domains of instructional strategies and the Instructional Strategy Flipbook.

Each component provides the reader with actionable steps to take that are proven to affect instructional practice in classrooms, enhance rigor of student thinking, improve student engagement, hone effective collaboration, and facilitate the selection of high-impact instructional moves.

So What? What are the implications for this chapter and your leadership framework? What are the implications of the research?

_____
_____
_____
_____

Now What? What will you do differently as a result?

_____
_____
_____
_____

4

THE INSTRUCTIONAL COACH'S ROLE IN TEACHER TEAMS AND PLCs

Instructional Coaches and Achievement Teams

The role of instructional coaches supporting teacher collaboration is not a new concept, but it's one that seems to have had varying degrees of success and implementation. In some instances, coaches are responsible for facilitating learning communities, guiding teams through a process of self-reflection and practice. In other instances, coaches are less of a facilitator and contribute more directly to the team's instructional success.

Either way, instructional coaches are catalysts for improving practice, and their expertise can support teachers in the reflective process required for effective teaching and learning. Furthermore, coaches who can help teachers develop evidence-based instructional practices can elevate teacher team success. What coaches should avoid most is simply teaching teachers how to conduct a collaborative protocol. Instead, effective coaches must be committed facilitators or consistently engaged participants during these protocols.

Education consultant and author Steve Barkley (2024) draws a clear distinction between professional *working* communities and professional *learning* communities. He notes that in many schools, teachers are engaged in activities called PLCs but are often something else—perhaps professional *working* communities (PWCs). However, when teams redirect their focus toward answering the question "What do students need *us* to *learn?*" they can effectively avoid the typical pitfalls of ineffective PLCs.

Why is this chapter important? Leaders who understand the essential role of instructional coaches in collaborative teacher teams better support continuous learning by modeling and facilitating effective teacher-driven conversations.

How can it improve your personal leadership profile? When principals partner with coaches, they send the message that, as a community, they promote trust and share ownership of supporting a positive coaching culture. Leaders can gain valuable insight into the role of coaches as they strive to meet teachers' needs. This means de-emphasizing the misconception that coaches "fix" teachers and emphasizing the idea that coaches focus on student needs.

PLC Pitfalls and How to Avoid Them

Sadly, many leaders know from experience that PLCs don't just fall into place. Implementation requires thoughtful action and leadership. Without thoughtfulness, you run the risk of creating PLCs that are ineffective wastes of time with the potential to have a negative impact on school culture. Here are some signs that your PLCs are in need of stronger instructional leadership—and some antidotes to address those pitfalls.

Pitfall 1: There is a lack of clarity, cohesion, and alignment after meetings and in classrooms.

Leadership Antidote: Establish structure. Clarify expectations for PLC meetings and team members. Equip teams with proven structured protocols, like the Achievement Teams protocol, to create cohesion.

Pitfall 2: Team members are often late to, absent from, or distracted during PLC meetings.
Leadership Antidote: Ensure commitment. Establish PLC roles, such as facilitator and recorder, and involve team members in cocreating a shared vision for what PLC time will look and feel like. Revisit these commitments in each PLC meeting to identify strengths and areas for improvement.

Pitfall 3: Leaders do not regularly attend or participate in PLCs, and/or there is evident instructional misalignment across grade levels and classrooms.
Leadership Antidote: Lead. Attend PLC meetings regularly, support facilitation where needed, and help develop your teacher leaders through the process. Gather feedback regularly regarding how you can best support PLC work.

Pitfall 4: Student achievement remains stagnant and there is little focus on concrete data.
Leadership Antidote: Prioritize data. Ensure that every PLC meeting leverages reliable protocols and short-cycle assessments to keep a laserlike focus on student work and performance.

Achievement Teams maintain the position that ongoing assessment provides the information teachers need to accurately identify what students need. Instructional coaches are essential in further promoting this thinking. When leaders focus on creating high-functioning, collaborative PLCs, they amplify their impact across multiple classrooms and have the potential to improve academic outcomes for more students (Ventura, 2024).

The Impact of Instructional Coaching

According to Hattie (2023), there is an effect size for instructional coaching. For clarity, an effect size measures the difference between two average means, typically comparing a treatment group to a nontreatment group (commonly referred to as a control group). This measurement is called Cohen's *d,* as effect sizes are classified as small (*d* = 0.2), medium (*d* = 0.5), and large (*d* ≥0.8).

The effect size for instructional coaching currently sits at 0.26, suggesting that there may not be too much of a difference between teachers who receive coaching and teachers who do not. However, there is much more to consider than just the final effect, which is an aggregate score of several effects.

One reason for this seemingly low effect size is that there were only 88 pieces of research data available that involved 8,099 people. Hattie argues that low effect sizes do not necessarily mean low impact. Rather, we need additional studies to raise the confidence of this finding.

Coaching is shown to have the strongest effect on the following teaching behaviors: learning attitudes, self-efficacy beliefs, skill acquisition, and teaching practice (see Figure 4.1). Let's take a closer look at each of these findings and analyze their individual and collective impact.

Coaches Improve Learning Attitudes

Great coaches can shift teachers' perspectives, helping them realize their full potential. In addition, coaches can increase positive teacher emotions by

FIGURE 4.1

Coaching Impact on Teaching Behaviors Effect Sizes

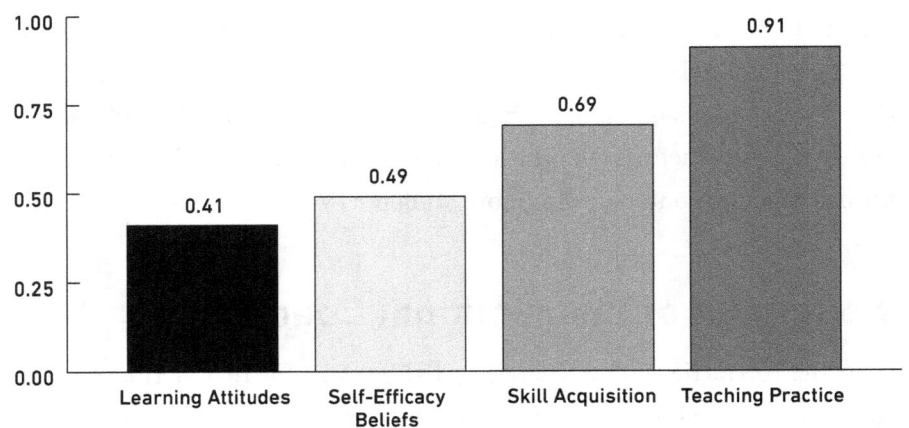

creating a no-fault reflection process in which teachers learn from mistakes, enabling them to experiment with instructional strategies they may not be familiar with. Learning attitudes are often the result of prior teaching experiences. Depending on those experiences, coaches can address successes and challenges and create an environment of ongoing discovery. Most important, coaches help teachers become excited, energized, and better able to meet their students' needs.

Learning attitudes can take on a number of different forms, but they are all within a coach's range of support. The most well-known learning attitude is a growth mindset. Carol Dweck (2016) defines *growth mindset* as the belief that one's abilities, intelligence, and talents are not fixed traits but can be developed over time through effort, learning, and perseverance. Other learning attitudes include empathy, the ability to receive and use feedback to increase instructional success, and being open to new ideas (e.g., innovative teaching strategies).

Some of the more traditional methods to increase positive learning attitudes include modeling, providing feedback, and engaging in learning labs. However, coaches can also assume the role of change agent by focusing on instructionally centered interactions with teachers. The partnerships coaches form with teachers should never be based on evaluation. Teachers need to know that developing a working relationship with a coach means that observations and feedback are purely designed to increase their ability to deliver highly effective instruction. Likewise, leaders need to know that coaches are not assigned to "fix" teachers or place them on an improvement plan. Doing so would almost ensure that being coached would be the last thing any teacher would want.

One of the better definitions of what instructional coaches do comes from Joellen Killion (n.d.), who describes instructional coaching as a way to develop and refine teaching: "Instructional coaches are on-site professional developers who teach educators how to use proven instructional methods. To be successful in this role, coaches must be skilled in a variety of roles, including public relations guru, communicator extraordinaire, master organizer, and, of course, expert educator" (p. 3).

Coaches Improve Self-Efficacy Beliefs

Many educators are familiar with the term *collective teacher efficacy*. If you are familiar with any of Hattie's *Visible Learning* publications, you probably recognize this as the primary effect size. Collective teacher efficacy is "the perceptions of teachers in a school that the efforts of faculty as a whole will have a positive effect on students" (Goddard et al., 2000, p. 480). However, teacher self-efficacy is slightly different from collective teacher efficacy. Teacher self-efficacy is a teacher's confidence in their ability to promote students' learning (Hoy, 2000).

In his review of the research, Jerald (2007) highlights the behaviors related to a teacher's sense of self-efficacy. Teachers with a strong sense of efficacy

- Tend to exhibit greater levels of planning, organization, and collaboration.
- Are more open to new ideas and willing to experiment with new methods to better meet their students' needs.
- Are more persistent and resilient when things do not go smoothly.
- Are less critical of students when they make errors.
- Are less likely to refer students to special education.

Coaches increase teacher self-efficacy by providing instructional support during PLCs or Achievement Teams meetings. They can

- Assist in goal setting between pre- and post-assessments.
- Provide support for all team members or drill down to a personalized support system.
- Introduce and model instructional strategies associated with high-yield impact.
- Focus on student learning.
- Encourage teachers to share their master experiences (a particular lesson that was a success in terms of instructional outcomes and student engagement), therefore influencing vicarious experiences of others on the team (i.e., motivating other teachers to have the same success).

Coaches Improve Skill Acquisition

This finding is based on evidence that shows the benefits of incorporating microteaching/learning labs, simulated instructional practices, and mentoring into the coaching regimen. These are among the most important teacher preparation practices and also seem ideal for instructional coaches who support teacher collaboration.

Jim Knight (2013) advocates for the use of video (of teaching in action) as a powerful tool to improve professional learning. This is commonly referred to as microteaching, which we will explore further in Chapter 6. Even if the video of our own instructional practices leaves us feeling disappointed—due to being hypercritical of our own performance—video helps capture teacher and student moves and moments that coaches might otherwise miss.

So how can coaches improve skill acquisition? This book contains several instructional strategies for teachers to consider using, but to make those strategies even more effective, coaches should encourage teachers to adapt to new skills and methods, all while keeping a focus on experimentation—not perfection.

Coaches Improve Teaching Practice

This finding is considered the primary purpose of coaching Achievement Teams and PLCs. If school- and district-level leaders are fortunate enough to have instructional coaches, they need to provide them with the necessary support, consider them to be instructional specialists, and encourage them to collaborate with teachers and assist with lesson design.

The implications for classroom practice are based on the team's analysis of assessment data. Teaching practice is widely viewed as an area in which leaders do not typically micromanage instruction. However, coaches know that there are certain instructional practices that work better than others in various situations, and leaders need to tap a coach's expertise to realize the power of this particular effect size. The 0.91 effect size associated with teaching practice is considered to be large, so the instructional strategies teachers choose to help close achievement gaps should be of the highest quality and designed to raise students' levels of thinking and learning around specific learning intentions.

The Three Coaching Stages

When these findings on the effectiveness of teaching practices were published, Jim Knight (2019) used them to categorize coaching into three stages with an intentional connection to Visible Learning:

1. The **identify stage** includes a clear picture of reality, including strategies to meet student-focused goals.
2. The **learn stage** is when the coach helps prepare teachers to attain the goal by clearly describing the strategy to be implemented.
3. The **improve stage** is when the coach supports the teacher as they adapt until the goal is attained.

Coaching Stage 1: Identify

Teachers must understand what teaching should look like in their classrooms before any goals are established. Specifically, microteaching can give teachers a sense of student engagement, clarifying the amount of time measured between monologue (teacher talk) and dialogue (increased student voice). Learning intentions and success criteria, which have a very high effect and probability in significantly advancing student achievement, should also be used. For example, a teacher selects the following learning target and would like to use it with students as it represents an important student-focused goal: *Determine two or more central ideas in a text and analyze their development over the course of the text; provide an objective summary of the text.*

In order to have students engage with this target, the teacher restates the goal (standard) in student-friendly language, which is commonly referred to as the learning intention:

- In this unit, you will learn how to find more than one central idea in a text and explain how the ideas develop throughout the text.
- In this unit, you will learn how to give an unbiased summary of a piece of informational text.

Keep in mind that the learning intention does not need to contain every detail from the original standard; it just needs to retain the essence of what the standard says. The specific details will be included in the success criteria, which the teacher and coach develop together as a series of "I can" statements, with an eye toward how to achieve the learning intention:

- I can determine two central ideas of the text.
- I can identify two to three key details for each central idea.
- I can analyze the details to explain how they support the central ideas.
- I can explain where in the text the central ideas are developed.
- I can formulate an objective summary of the text, including the most important ideas and details about the topic.

Hattie (2023) says, "The purpose of success criteria, or *we are successful when,* is to make students understand what the teacher uses as the destination or notion of mastery" (p. 313). To that end, instructional coaches can help cocreate success criteria with teachers, which sparks an exchange of ideas. Leaders need to understand that clearly articulated success criteria can lead to better feedback between teachers and students. This feedback should be directly connected to the success criteria—highlighting what was done well and identifying areas for improvement. In this way, success criteria not only help create focus for students but also provide them with meaningful opportunities to recognize their strengths and target areas of need. Above all, coaches must help teachers purposefully link success criteria to a specific learning target so students can demonstrate that they can monitor their own progress.

Coaching Stage 2: Learn

In this stage, coaches explain the strategy with precision and clarity. The goal is not only to create success criteria but also to have students interact with the criteria. The wonderful thing about using success criteria is that there are multiple ways to create and implement them. There's no one right way, as long as the criteria shared with students represent high expectations for learning.

One method coaches can use to assist teachers with student engagement around success criteria is to incorporate the use of a detail wheel (see Figure 4.2). Detail wheels are simple to make and foster high levels of student engagement. Teachers place the learning intention in the center of the wheel

FIGURE 4.2
Detail Wheel

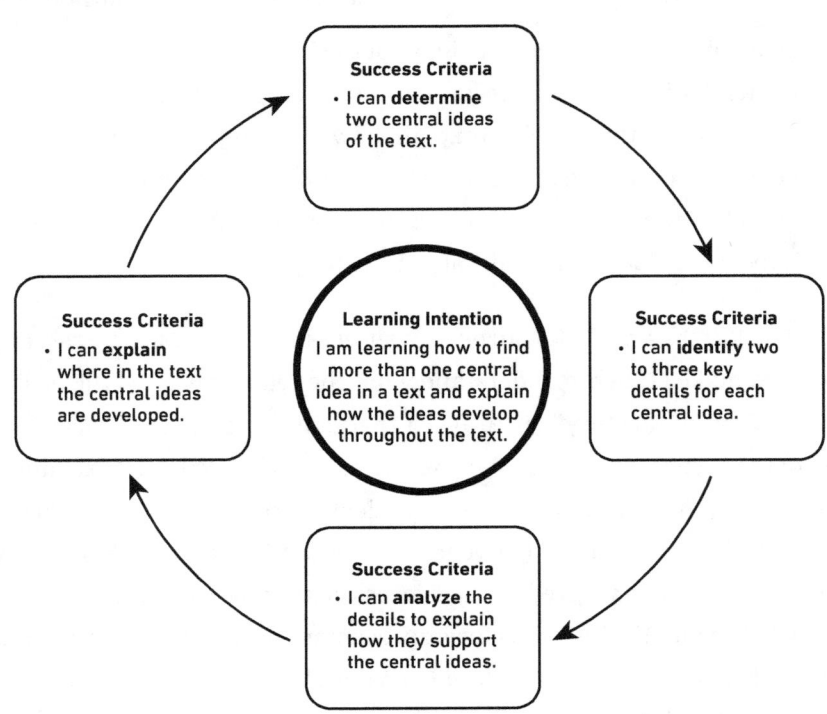

and then introduce the success criteria, one at a time, around the wheel. In other words, teachers should not introduce new success criteria until there is a specified goal or mastery level based on the previously introduced criteria, accompanied by feedback to students about their progress identifying what has been achieved and what still needs improvement. Of course, when this happens is based on the teacher's judgment and observations, but if a large portion of the classroom is able to determine two central ideas, for example, the teacher can then reveal the next criterion by having students identify key ideas for each central idea.

This practice has a high probability of making a difference in the classroom. When instructional coaches work with teacher teams to collectively create success criteria, the outcomes are highly effective on learning regardless of students' home life, demographics, or socioeconomic status. As teachers and coaches create learning intentions and success criteria, their collective ability strengthens and promotes better outcomes for students.

Developing learning intentions and success criteria allows teachers to align their instruction with assessments. It also helps narrow the focus of instruction by identifying what matters most to student learning. By implementing learning intentions and success criteria in the classroom, educators can inspire their students to become self-regulated learners. The impact is significant, with students performing up to two times more proficiently than students who rely on teacher support. It's worth repeating that success criteria provide the way of knowing that the desired learning (learning intention) has been achieved (Hattie, 2009).

Coaching Stage 3: Improve

After identifying a clear picture of current reality and the ways teachers can learn to use appropriate strategies, we can move on to the final coaching stage. In this stage, coaches support teachers in effectively employing instructional strategies, especially if an implemented strategy was not successful. This is critical since teacher teams need coaches who can suggest other high-leverage instructional strategies or modify the ones they have selected.

With respect to learning intentions and success criteria, adaptations are essential. If success criteria are not clearly articulated, students may not refer to those criteria as they reflect on their own progress. In the following example, the teacher has determined that the chosen strategy is correct, but the implementation needs to be modified. Therefore, the teacher and coach work together to determine additional strategies so students are maximizing the use of success criteria. The coach then models how to

- Coconstruct success criteria with students. Students who help create success criteria are more likely to refer to them. This can be accomplished through the use of rubrics and scoring guides.
- Display success criteria where they are visible throughout the entire lesson(s) and referred to often.
- Communicate success criteria to students using appropriate language.
- Use examples and nonexamples of success criteria so students can determine which criteria are most appropriate.

- Use error analysis, where students must assess a sample piece of work that contains errors, then refer to the success criteria to correct those errors.

The three coaching stages provide coaches with a strong road map and effective model to use while improving collaboration, instructional strategies, and the application of the findings from Visible Learning. Leaders and coaches are encouraged to create conditions where the probability of yielding high effects is present throughout the entire coaching and collaborative process. When leaders ask instructional coaches to guide PLCs, what they should really be asking is how can coaching a PLC "help everyone get the most out of these powerful professional learning structures" (Sweeney & Harris, 2020, p. 18).

Achievement Teams are focused on evidence from high-quality short-cycle assessments and use achievement groups to help determine intervention strategies. Formative, ongoing assessment occurs in many schools and districts. However, the results of those assessments may not lead to elevated levels of student progress. This outcome can only occur when teachers and coaches understand that formative assessment is designed to assist teachers in evaluating their instructional impact.

Coaches Ask the Right Questions

In a *Harvard Business Review* article, Chevallier and colleagues (2024) explore questioning techniques to drive better decision making. Some of the techniques they explored involved a question mix under four domains (or styles): speculative questions, productive questions, interpretive questions, and investigative questions. These question types are designed to reduce a social dynamic called *pluralistic ignorance*, a phenomenon wherein team members fail to share mistakes or vulnerabilities because no one else is doing so.

A more straightforward example of this is when people are worried about coming up with the correct answer, so they hold back out of fear of looking unintelligent, especially if their answer is incorrect. Some people avoid sharing their best thinking altogether so they won't be put in that position. If these scenarios sound familiar, you may be making a connection between this dynamic and your own collaborative team meetings. If members of a PLC avoid sharing challenges, then PLCs have lost their intent of inclusivity, professional autonomy, and collaboration.

Instructional coaches can adapt the use of these questions to help navigate around passive team members or a lack of equitable contributions from the entire team. Many instructional coaches already incorporate the use of "question storming," or brainstorming for questions rather than answers. This is similar to root cause analysis, where the goal is not to come up with an answer but to discover opportunities that exist. With this in mind, leaders should encourage coaches to ask questions that promote critical thinking, collaboration, and continuous improvement. The most effective questions can also help coaches build trust, strengthen relationships, and create a positive and supportive school culture.

Let's take a look at the four questioning techniques coaches can use while they support teachers in determining instructional strategies (see Figure 4.3). The emphasis here is on teacher actions that affect student learning and performance.

FIGURE 4.3
Four Questioning Techniques

Speculative	Productive	Interpretive	Investigative
These questions help consider the issue more broadly, reframe it, overcome limiting assumptions, and explore more creative solutions.	This kind of question helps assess the availability of talent, capabilities, time, and other resources.	Sensemaking questions such as these push coaches to continually redefine the core issue and ask what the problem is really about.	Effective coaches start by finding out what they need to learn in order to accomplish their coaching goal.
How could we increase the use of menus and other independent learning strategies?	*How can we break down this lesson into smaller chunks of learning?*	*What did you learn from the pre-assessment results? Were there any patterns associated with student responses?*	*Can you describe an instructional strategy you use that demonstrates consistent positive results?*
What might happen if we tried incorporating more reflective learning strategies in your lesson (e.g., error analysis, inquiry writing)?	*What resources are available to specifically address some of the learning gaps in your classroom?*	*What are some reasons for various student engagement levels?*	*What areas of your teaching do you feel you need to improve in order to be more effective?*

Source: Inspired by content from "The Art of Asking Smarter Questions," by A. Chevallier, F. Dalsace, and J.-L. Barsoux, 2024, *Harvard Business Review, 102*(3), p. 66–74.

As you can see, these questions are designed to increase curiosity and self-reflection. In my experience, schools that promote a reflective teaching culture see a significant increase in both teacher and student performance. Reflective teaching provides a powerful way to achieve this by fostering professional growth, improving teaching practices, and enhancing student outcomes.

Coaches who help teachers examine their own teaching methods and strategies typically pose self-reflective questions such as these:

- What am I doing in the classroom?
- Why am I doing it this way?
- Is it effective for student learning?

Some leaders may not be familiar with how to maximize their instructional coaches' impact, especially during teacher collaboration time. A central pillar of effective school leadership is their active promotion of and participation in teacher learning and development, including the principal–coach partnership. Research consistently shows that when school leaders engage directly in professional development alongside their staff, it not only enhances their credibility but also significantly boosts the overall quality of teaching. According to a study from the Institute of Education Sciences, leaders who model continuous learning and provide opportunities for staff development can double the impact on student achievement, with an effect size of 0.84 (Irwin, 2023).

Leader Action Step: Start by scheduling regular, informal learning sessions where you, as a leader, join teachers and instructional coaches in discussions about new teaching strategies or share insights from recent professional development experiences. This not only reinforces the value of professional growth but also creates a culture where learning is a shared journey. For instance, you could initiate monthly learning labs in which teachers experiment with new methods in a supportive setting, with you and the instructional coach actively participating and providing feedback. These labs could occur during after-school programming time, intervention blocks, or elective and special classes. This simple step can help bridge the gap among leadership, coaching, and teaching, thereby fostering a stronger, more collaborative school environment.

Coach Action Step: Coaches can use PLC time to establish Achievement Teams that facilitate collaborative planning among teacher teams. These teams should meet regularly to review and develop curriculum plans, assess the effectiveness of teaching strategies, and make necessary adjustments. Encourage team members to share best practices and provide constructive feedback. By actively involving themselves in these meetings, coaches demonstrate their commitment to continuous improvement and set a standard for collaborative leadership in the school (Dunst et al., 2019).

"What? So What? Now What?" Critical Reflection Model

What? In this chapter, we explored the following key ideas related to an instructional coach's role in collaborative teacher teams:

1. Attuning to and addressing common PLC pitfalls.
2. The proven impact of instructional coaching on teachers' learning attitudes, self-efficacy beliefs, and instructional practice.
3. Effectively navigating the three coaching stages (Identify, Learn, Improve).
4. The power of asking the right questions.

With these skills and tools added to the instructional coaching toolkit, leaders can fully activate and catalyze the immense power of effective teacher collaboration, using PLCs and Achievement Teams to streamline instructional improvement and establish a culture of continuous learning.

So What? What are the implications for this chapter and your leadership framework? What are the implications of the research?

_____

_____

_____

_____

Now What? What will you do differently as a result?

_____
_____
_____
_____

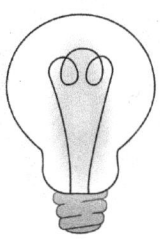

5

INDICATORS OF EFFECTIVE COLLABORATION

Five Profiles of Focused Collaboration

To begin discussing the indicators of effective collaboration, it's critical to explore the foundation for effective teacher teams and the processes they use to improve instructional practice. In my previous book, *Achievement Teams* (Ventura & Ventura, 2022), my co-author and I outlined specific behaviors that are value-added practices when teachers collaborate. Here, I take a more focused approach by explaining the five profiles of effective collaboration and how to lead these practices. These five profiles, when combined, can help teams reach goals and learning targets with a high degree of success. We will examine all five of these elements and how they make a difference in a team's collaborative effectiveness.

1. Facilitate a well-defined structure for successful collaboration.
2. Understand that assessment results reflect instructional effort.
3. Use assessment results and data to explicitly make informed decisions based on evidence.

4. Create relational trust so teams can operate at an optimal level.
5. Lead change in PLCs.

Why is this chapter important? Leaders must be willing to implement the necessary steps to create and promote effective collaboration. The steps included in this chapter promote a collaborative protocol that fosters resilience among staff and students.

How can it improve your personal leadership profile? The leadership elements contained in this chapter, including self-reflection, innovation, and coaching, enable school leaders to clearly set expectations for collaboration while promoting a clearly defined structure. In turn, this will positively influence staff culture and nurture continuous learning.

As each element is unpacked, leaders will be able to develop a monitoring plan (see Figure 5.1) to ensure that change initiatives are consistently implemented. Remember, change initiatives that are moderate and inconsistent are no better than implementation that was completely absent. The Leadership Thinking Prompts (Figure 5.2) encourage introspection on your current understanding of instructional leadership.

Facilitate a Well-Defined Structure for Successful Collaboration

In successful collaboration, team members are committed to facilitating a well-defined structure in pursuit of success. Instructional leadership is a shared responsibility, but there are some aspects of leadership that are the sole responsibility of either the principal or central office administrator. These leaders need to get out in front and create a framework for collaboration that is not only organized but also instructionally effective.

Collaborative discussions can be extremely powerful and effective. However, if there is a gap in participation—a lack of focus and no accountability—a PLC can become confusing with a heavy dose of frustration. There is extensive research that suggests that PLC collaboration positively influences student achievement. However, the most obvious challenge is the gap

FIGURE 5.1
Monitoring Plan

Profiles	1: Nonpracticing: This has not yet been established.	2: Initial stages: We are starting to take action.	3: Progressing: There are small pockets of success.	4: Partial: implementation This cannot be considered common practice.	5: Fully implemented: This is common practice in our school.
Facilitate a well-defined structure for successful collaboration.					
Understand that assessment results reflect instructional effort.					
Use assessment results and data to explicitly make informed decisions based on evidence.					
Create relational trust so teams can operate at an optimal level.					
Lead change in PLCs.					

Indicators of Effective Collaboration

FIGURE 5.2
Leadership Thinking Prompts

Reflect on each of these prompts to explore your current understanding of instructional leadership and the role of a leader in teacher teams. Think of specific examples for each.

1. How do teachers use assessment data when making decisions about instruction?

2. Do teams build relational trust so collaboration can occur under the most positive conditions? How so?

3. When data are analyzed, how can team members be encouraged to go deeper in determining root causes?

4. How often do teams get an opportunity to truly work collectively to create common goals designed to increase student learning?

between the positive aspects of PLC collaboration and actual implementation (Cornell University, 2024).

In *10 Mindframes for Visible Learning,* Hattie and Zierer (2018) outline mindframes that promote teachers as evaluators and offer a way of thinking that should underpin every action in schools. One key mindframe tied to student achievement is an educator's belief that student assessment results are a direct reflection of their own teaching—not of student effort. This concept may require leaders to pivot teachers away from seeing assignments and assessments as the result of student effort and toward understanding that the results of those assessments are a direct reflection of the teacher's efforts. This can be an uncomfortable truth but one that can be explained. We will unpack this further later in this chapter.

Ideally, teacher collaboration allows teachers to develop new skills while addressing strengths and gaps in student learning. I often refer to PLCs as learning labs and work with teams to provide a structure for collaboration: the Achievement Teams process (Ventura & Ventura, 2022). That process takes the guesswork out of collaborative meetings and involves a four-step meeting protocol with a continuous cycle. The structure is simple yet effective and has proven to be beneficial in hundreds of schools. Beyond providing teacher teams and leaders with a predictable structure that greatly affects student achievement, the Achievement Teams process also supports educators in embracing the essential mindframe of owning student data and viewing it as a reflection of instructional effort.

Achievement Teams Four-Step Meeting Protocol

Step 1: Collect and chart the data. Achievement Teams focus on evidence from high-quality short-cycle assessments.

Step 2: Set SMART goals. Creating goals for both students and teachers has a tremendous effect on academic outcomes.

Step 3: Create baseline evidence statements. Summarizing collected data helps educators make inferences around students' mastery levels.

Step 4: Select high-yield instructional strategies. Teachers select the strategies that will have the greatest effect on student achievement.

This protocol allows leaders to provide teachers with as much support as possible, especially in light of increased demands to indicate student progress and achievement. It also allows teachers to be creative, sharing their past experiences and successes. During my four years as a district superintendent, I was determined to make sure there was no confusion about why teachers were meeting. The goals of every meeting remained the same: discuss, evaluate, reflect, and adjust instructional strategies. I was adamant that instruction must be aligned to assessment results and other quantifiable measures of evidence. Without making this crystal clear, we risk the possibility of perpetuating and even amplifying the status quo.

Overall, this protocol provides a structure for teachers to accurately reflect on teaching between pre- and post-assessments while simultaneously identifying areas of student need. Teachers then collaboratively decide on the best corrective instructional approach in response to those needs. When schools and districts de-emphasize individual practice and promote collective ability, they create professional teams of educators who continuously reflect on and improve their practice. See Figure 5.3 to gain a better understanding of the structure I recommend for school teams.

Reflect on Your Current Collaboration

Review the Achievement Teams Success Criteria in Figure 5.3 and reflect on the following prompts.

1. Do your current collaborative teams get to this level of rigorous collaborative discourse?

   _____
   _____
   _____

2. Based on these criteria, where do teams need to improve?

   _____
   _____
   _____

3. Explain your current level of team dialogue.

   _____
   _____
   _____

4. What areas need to improve in order to encourage deeper levels of teacher self-reflection?

   _____
   _____
   _____

FIGURE 5.3
Achievement Teams Success Criteria

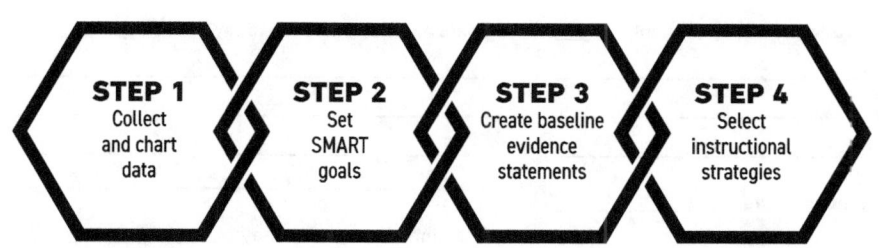

STEP 1: Collect/Chart Assessment Results
a) Results include number of students at multiple performance levels (i.e., excelling, achieving, progressing, beginning).
b) Results are organized in the Achievement Teams spreadsheet before the start of meeting.
c) Results include student work samples from the assessment.
d) Results will provide specific feedback to students and teachers about skills and concepts that students achieved and those that still need to be learned.

STEP 2: Establish SMART Goals
a) Goals are established based on students' current levels of proficiency using a growth formula or teacher professional judgement.
b) SMART goals are shared with students.
c) Students set individual goals between pre- and post-assessment.
d) Achievable gains in student learning take into account the current performance of all students and/or are based on the use of a growth formula.
e) An agreed-upon time is set for the administration of the post-assessment.

STEP 3: Create Baseline Evidence Statements
a) Teams make inferences regarding student progress by analyzing pre-assessment results.
b) Evidence statements and needs identified are within the direct influence of teachers.
c) Conversations are purposeful and are based on the four Achievement Teams focus questions: What strengths and gaps do the assessment results show? What skills (verbs) and concepts (nouns and noun phrases) were achieved from the learning target, and what still needs to be learned? Who did we teach effectively, and who still needs help? Which instructional strategies were effective, and which were less effective?
d) Teams identify root causes based on where students are in the learning progressions and on the pre-assessment results.

STEP 4: Select Instructional Strategies
a) Strategies directly target the strengths and gaps identified during Step 3: Create Baseline Evidence Statements.
b) Teams describe and choose research-based strategies (for each performance group, if possible).
c) Teachers prioritize high-impact strategies to use between the pre- and post-assessments.
d) Strategies selected will improve teachers' instructional delivery and practice.
e) Teams agree that strategies selected are high yield and high impact.

(continued)

FIGURE 5.3
Achievement Teams Success Criteria (*continued*)

Grade Level/Department: _____
_____
_____
_____

Meeting Date: _____

Assessment: _____

Team Members: _____
_____
_____
_____
_____
_____
_____
_____
_____

Goals and outcomes for today's meeting: _____
_____
_____
_____
_____

Questions to explore today: _____
_____
_____
_____

Actions we need to take: _____
_____
_____
_____

Strategies to try: _____
_____
_____
_____

Ideas for the next team meeting: _____
_____
_____
_____
_____

Notes: _____
_____
_____
_____
_____

Understand That Assessment Results Reflect Instructional Effort

In *Visible Learning: The Sequel,* John Hattie (2023) explains the importance of formative assessment and evaluation, which can accelerate student learning. However, Hattie outlines some common misconceptions about assessment, starting with the confusion that exists between formative assessment and testing. He asserts that assessment, whether it be formative or summative, is not as important as the way the results are evaluated. In fact, Black and Wiliam (1998) conclude that classroom assessment typically encourages superficial and rote learning, concentrating on the recall of isolated details that students soon forget. "Teachers do not generally review the assessment questions that they use and do not discuss them critically with peers, so there is little reflection on what is being assessed" (p. 18).

Teachers and leaders need to talk about the quality of the evidence and the nature of formative evaluation. Incorporating these aspects leads to better decision making. In many cases, assessments are typically used for grading rather than determining if instruction is effective. Furthermore, many learning environments are focused solely on testing—to the exclusion of learning—perpetuating a tendency to only judge student performance levels without identifying the antecedents of results, the instructional root causes that lead to achievement. In the late 1960s, Benjamin Bloom (1968) recognized that the assessments most teachers use serve mainly as a way to confirm for which students the teachers' instruction was appropriate and for which it wasn't.

Without leadership clarity regarding the purpose of assessment, the basics of assessment literacy, and the possible misinterpretation of results, teachers tend to focus on students who are closer to attaining learning targets and less on those who have more room to grow. To mitigate these results, leaders can use the following suggestions to keep assessments on track.

Leaders must be clear about the use and purpose of formative assessment by explaining how assessments are to be used and how they closely relate to learning targets. In many of the schools I work with, teachers administer district benchmark assessments with no feedback about student performance and no time to discuss results. Clearly articulating the goals and objectives of formative assessment can greatly reduce misconceptions and confusion.

In addition, there are many different types of assessments, from project-based to formative and summative assessments. To accurately learn more about students' strengths and needs, leaders must emphasize the most appropriate assessment for the content being assessed. For example, I recommend short-cycle assessments to help teachers focus on the formative effects of their teaching.

In brief, formative assessment should

1. Inform teacher practice.
2. Promote equity for all students.
3. Build the capacity of all team members.
4. Provide an effective strategy to determine if students have achieved the learning targets.
5. Offer a powerful tool to appropriate new knowledge about teaching and learning.
6. Encourage students to become better consumers of their own learning (Ventura & Ventura, 2022, p. 53).

One of the best ways to clarify the purpose of assessment is through ongoing professional development, where teachers have opportunities to discuss assessment strategies, which leads to better understanding and practice. I use a simple form to help teachers design assessments—or at least make sure the assessments they use are set at the correct level of cognitive demand and rigor. This three-step process is powerful yet simple to use, and once teachers understand the protocol, leaders can be assured of an increased understanding of assessment design and administration.

This assessment strategy analysis follows three steps:

1. Determine the prioritized learning target.
2. Unwrap the learning target to determine skills (verbs) and concepts (nouns).
3. Determine the assessment item type based on rigor and cognitive demand.

Figure 5.4 includes a sample template that demonstrates all three parts. The learning target is a high-priority English language arts standard that includes three key skills and concepts.

First, the standard is written out to denote the skills and concepts, indicated by using bold text for the verbs (skills) and underlining the noun or noun phrases (concepts). In this particular example, *determine, analyze,* and *provide an objective summary (summarize)* are the skills.

FIGURE 5.4
Formative Assessment Planning Template Example

Unit Title/Focus	Grade Level/Course	Authors	Date
ELA	Grade 10	Steve V.	May 17

Step 1: Determine priority standard

LITERACY.RI.10.2:
Determine a central idea of a text and **analyze** its development over the course of the text, including how it emerges and is shaped and refined by specific details; **provide an objective summary** of the text.

Step 2: Unwrap standard to identify skills and concepts

Skills (Verbs) – what students will do	**Concepts (Nouns)** – what students need to know
Determine	a central idea of a text
Analyze	its development over the course of the text
Summarize	the text

Step 3: Determine assessment item types using skills from standard

Determine (Level 2—Skill/Concept) = **Selected response** (multiple choice, true/false, matching, fill in the blank. **Short answer** (generally one paragraph, writing a list, steps in a process)

Analyze (Level 3—Strategic Thinking) = **Nontraditional Selected Response** (can have two correct answers). **Extended Response** (multi-paragraph, may have multiple answers/solutions, includes justification); pair with another item for justification.

Summarize (Level 2—Skill/Concept) = **Short constructed response** (one-paragraph summary).

Next, the standard is unwrapped by separating the skills and the concepts. The skills are on the left side and the concepts are on the right. Unwrapping standards is certainly not a new technique, but it is an important piece when educators need to identify those key elements that students should master. Moreover, breaking down a learning target can ensure that assessments are aligned with what needs to be taught, as this framework demonstrates. The more targeted the instruction, the more classroom teachers can focus on the most important concepts. Unwrapped standards also provide the foundation for a clearly articulated curriculum that creates consistency about what should be taught across all classrooms.

Finally, the skills and concepts within the learning target must be assessed based on the elements within the standard and matched with the correct assessment attributes. Figure 5.5 breaks down each Depth of Knowledge (DOK) level by including learner actions, key actions, and the application to assessments. This tool helps reduce deficit instruction and assessment by suggesting the type of assessment format that matches each skill.

Properly Using Depth of Knowledge

It is important to note that DOK focuses on the complexity of cognitive processes required to complete a task, not just the skill itself. The verbs contained in many state standards provide surface-level suggestions for where the actual DOK levels can be determined. As Karin Hess explained to me,

> To apply DOK properly, consider the mental processing required to determine a central idea in a text—for many informational texts, this is often less complex than identifying and supporting interpretations of themes in literary texts. Literary texts generally require more nuanced interpretations because of literary devices or discourse styles used, for example. Determining central ideas of informational texts requires at least a cursory knowledge of the content of the entire text (such as when summarizing) and informational texts often have introductory paragraphs with overviews (e.g., "This article presents three reasons why . . .") or text features like subheadings that act as signposts pointing readers to ideas that will be presented. Informational texts with more complex or abstract concepts (e.g., dystopia) require deeper levels of processing than those presenting more familiar or straightforward ideas. (personal communication, 2024)

FIGURE 5.5

Application of Depth of Knowledge to Assessments

Level	Learner Actions	Key Actions	Application to Assessments
Level 1: Acquire Foundation	Requires simple recall of information such as a fact, definition, term, or simple procedure.	List, Tell, Define, Label, Identify, Name, State, Write, Locate, Find, Match, Measure, Repeat	**Attributes:** One correct answer; recall; recognize; or define terms or properties **Selected Response** • Multiple choice • True/False; Yes/No • Matching • Fill in the blank **Short Constructed Response** • Listing • Short paragraph • Problem with work shown
Level 2: Use, Connect, and Conceptualize	Involves some mental skills, concepts, or processing; students must make some decisions about how to approach a problem or activity.	Estimate, Compare, Organize, Interpret, Modify, Predict, Cause/Effect, Summarize, Graph, Classify	**Attributes:** One correct answer applying multiple concepts and skills; may explain process/procedures **Selected Response** • Multiple choice • True/False; Yes/No • Matching • Graphic organizers (compare and contrast) **Short Constructed Response** • Generally one paragraph or less; writing a list; steps in a process
Level 3: Construct and Deepen Meaning	Requires reasoning, planning, using evidence, and thinking at a higher level.	Critique, Formulate, Hypothesize, Construct, Revise, Investigate, Differentiate, Compare-Contrast, Analyze	**Attributes:** May have multiple answers/solutions, includes justification **Nontraditional Selected Response** • Can have two correct answers • Can be paired with another item for justification of thinking **Short Constructed Response** • Can be paired with a selected response item • Problem with work shown/explanation of process **Extended Response** • Multiple-paragraph compositions drawing from a single source
Level 4: Extend, Transfer, and Broaden Meaning	Requires complex reasoning, planning, developing, and thinking. Cognitive demands are high; students are required to make connections both within and among subject domains.	Design, Connect, Synthesize, Apply, Critique, Analyze, Create, Prove, Support	**Attributes:** Extended time to complete and synthesis is required. *Multiple choice difficult to write at this level* **Extended Response** • Multiple-paragraph compositions using multiple sources • Apply a model to describe or design a mathematical model to inform or solve • Research projects/Performance-based assessment

It's important to point out what Depth of Knowledge is. To that end, DOK

- Is a language system that can differentiate between levels of complexity regarding how students engage with their educational materials.
- Can be used to interpret questions, prompts, tasks, standards, and learning objectives.
- Fosters intentionality in the way educators teach and helps ensure that the complexity of expectations is understood and that lessons include opportunities for students to engage at those levels.
- Helps us discern between complexity and difficulty.

Likewise, it's just as important to understand what DOK is *not*. It is not

- Used to evaluate the complexity of a topic or text.
- A rubric for measuring achievement.
- A measure of how students engage.
- A system to rate a learning progression from low to high complexity.
- A reflection of importance or value. In other words, one level of DOK isn't better than another.

With these explanations and definitions in mind (Klint, 2021), the assessment tool included here is designed to give educators suggested "clues" as to how students can engage with the skills embedded in standards and learning targets.

For example, the verb *analyze* has been identified as a suggested Level 3 skill (because it requires reasoning, planning, evidence, and thinking at a higher level). The type of assessment items recommended for this level of cognitive complexity could include the following strategies:

- **Nontraditional Selected Response:** can have two correct answers
- **Short Constructed Response:** can be paired with a selected response item
- **Extended Response:** multiple-paragraph compositions, may have multiple answers/solutions, includes justification, pair with another item for justification

Figure 5.6 includes a blank template you can use to plan your own formative assessments.

FIGURE 5.6
Formative Assessment Planning Template

Unit Title/Focus	Grade Level/Course	Authors	Date

Step 1: Determine priority standard

Step 2: Unwrap standard to identify skills and concepts	
Skills (Verbs) – what students will do	**Concepts (Nouns)** – what students need to know

Step 3: Determine assessment item types using skills from standard

Finally, the list of skills to be learned in Figure 5.7 is designed to further inform teachers on how to identify the correct DOK level.

When principals and other school leaders clearly identify the purpose of assessment and assessment criteria, they create the means for improving feedback to students while assessing the impact of teaching and learning. Don't assume that purchased curricula and curricular guides can address all areas of assessment; many of these publications assume that teachers and leaders have a solid understanding of assessment and learning targets. Using

FIGURE 5.7
Depth of Knowledge Levels, Observable Success Criteria (Engagement), and Content/Skills to be Learned

Level and Purpose	Success Criteria (from Novice to Expert) I/we can...
1: Acquire Foundation	• Follow specific steps to complete routine tasks. • Retrieve/locate/recall facts, details, and terms. • Use required tools/resources for specific purposes. • Practice and self-monitor routine skills/processes. • Perform routine operations; apply rules. • Recite/paraphrase definitions and principles.
2: Use, Connect, and Conceptualize	• Explain relationships (cause-effect; compare-contrast; if-then). • Organize or graph information. • Summarize, sequence, sort, classify, and infer. • Predict based on observations and prior knowledge. • Pose conceptual questions, problems, or topics to investigate. • Select and use tools/strategies for a specific purpose.
3: Construct and Deepen Meaning	• Uncover relevant, accurate, and credible information. • Reveal flaws in a design or claims. • Investigate questions that explore underlying/implied meanings. • Use criteria to evaluate or develop supporting evidence for conclusions, solutions, claims, or point of view. • Conduct, revise, and refine investigations. • Solve nonroutine problems. • Self-assess and reflect; use feedback to improve quality. • Make connections to big ideas or themes.
4: Extend, Transfer, and Broaden Meaning	• Initiate, transfer, and construct new knowledge. • Modify, create, elaborate, or evaluate based on analysis or integration of information from multiple sources. • Raise novel questions and investigate multifaceted real-world problems or issues. • Self-assess and reflect; use feedback to improve quality. • Develop broader insights linked to big ideas, essential questions, or themes.

Source: From *Applying Depth of Knowledge and Cognitive Rigor: An Educator's Guide to Supporting Deeper Learning,* by K. Hess, 2025, Teachers College Press. Copyright 2025 by Teachers College Press. Adapted with permission.

the process explained above sharpens focus, alignment, and purpose. It also improves reliability and validity, the cornerstone of effective assessment.

Formative Assessment and Grading

Before we move on to other leadership attributes, we need to address the misconception of grading assessments. This topic can be extremely emotional, but it's one that needs to be addressed. Guskey (2019) clearly states that avoiding grades can improve feedback, gauge instruction, support better understanding of barriers to growth, and monitor progress. Traditional grading is more appropriate for summative or end-of-course tests, but even then, it can be extremely subjective. Since this book is about leading and coaching PLCs, I won't delve too deep into the pitfalls of grading. However, I'll gently remind readers that grading an assessment is akin to academic malpractice. Feedback is more important than grading, especially when it is targeted and clearly linked to learning outcomes.

Since the assessments we are discussing should be focused and brief, leaders must be clear about how teachers and students use assessment results. To be clear, there may be occasional circumstances where a minimal grading component can be considered, but the primary purpose of assessment should be to provide timely feedback to students and reflective data analysis so teachers can focus on learning.

Use Assessment Results and Data to Explicitly Make Informed Decisions Based on Evidence

Data analysis is foundational to long-standing change in any field of work. In the classroom, the greatest supplier of data is assessments. However, assessments aren't just about evaluating students and the progress they are making; they're about changing what we are doing as educators to help students reach their goals.

The first step in that collaborative process is collecting, organizing, and charting quantitative data from formative assessment results. Although there are many sources of student achievement data, formative assessment results provide teachers with timely and specific feedback. This helps teacher teams collectively understand which concepts and skills have been learned and which still need to be developed. It is important to remember that the data teams collect cannot be so general that teachers are unable to assess their own instructional impact. The most useful assessments help teachers assess their impact and effect on student learning.

To that end, baseline evidence statements are summary statements derived from formative assessment results that help teachers make inferences about student performance levels. To arrive at these statements, teachers conduct a root cause analysis based on the pre-assessment results. The rich, collaborative discussions that ensue promote the core purpose of Achievement Teams: to continually assess our impact as teachers and leaders. This step is designed to help teachers reflect on their practice while enabling them to determine effective instructional strategies between the pre- and post-assessment.

For example, here are the four focus questions we ask Achievement Teams to consider as they analyze the data they collected:

1. What strengths and gaps do the assessment results show?
2. What skills (verbs) and concepts (nouns and noun phrases) were achieved from the learning target, and what still needs to be learned?
3. Who did we teach effectively, and who still needs help?
4. Which instructional strategies were effective, and which were less effective?

Facilitators should ask these questions to team members, reminding the team that the primary task is to understand that data and assessment results are a reflection of the teachers' instructional effort. To help visualize this process, I have included a data analysis scenario in Figure 5.8.

Another process for instructional decision making is based in part on the work of the Leadership for Urban Mathematics Project and the Assessment Communities of Teachers Project developed by Eric Buchovecky. The tool also draws on the work of Steve Seidel and Evangeline Harris-Stefanakis of Project Zero at Harvard University (Center for Leadership & Educational Equity, 2024). It is a systematic process for discussing data, as it compartmentalizes intentional discussions based on six steps. I adapted and modified this tool down to three steps in order to make discussions less time-consuming but still relevant. These steps also work well within the Achievement Teams model.

I recommend leaders incorporate a similar model, using three items for discussion that promote root cause analysis, self-reflection, and an awareness of what needs to be improved. Data analysis can be extremely dynamic,

FIGURE 5.8
Achievement Teams Discussions

Directions: Read the scenario and then discuss the questions that follow.

Scenario: A 6th grade team has charted their pre-assessment data and begins to discuss next steps. Ms. Morris states that she is very concerned about how her students performed and would like the team's help to determine a good plan for reteaching the skills within the learning target. Mr. Singh asks the team if they would like him to talk through the learning experiences he designed for his class prior to the pre-assessment. Ms. Nguyen comments that she would love to hear what Mr. Singh has been doing in class but that his strategies probably won't work in her class because her students struggle to focus and complete assigned tasks. Mr. Gutierrez suggests that the team take a closer look at the student data to identify trends in student performance. Ms. Lee asks, "How should we do that?" Five minutes before the end of the meeting, the team has yet to arrive on a plan to take collective action based on the pre-assessment data.

Pre-Assessment Data Sample

Teachers	Excelling	Achieving	Progressing	Beginning	Total Students
Singh	8	12	2	0	22
Morris	0	1	9	12	22
Gutierrez	0	3	11	7	21
Nguyen	0	10	10	3	23
Lee	0	4	16	0	20
Totals	8	30	48	22	108

What are some strengths of this team's conversation? How could this conversation have been different had this team used the focus questions to create baseline evidence statements?

_____
_____
_____
_____

Note: Scenario created by Elena Sammon and Angela Buckingham. Used with permission.

meaning that the results of the assessment provide teachers with real-time evidence while helping to determine areas of need and support.

Data Discussion Step 1: Description of the Data Being Analyzed

Here, teams describe in rich detail what they see as opposed to what needs to be done. This means that we isolate the difference between what we see and the opinions that may arise out of the data collected. Opinions and interpretation come later, after the team has exhausted all patterns of data. The benefits of such analysis permit focused conversations that highlight trends in assessment. The purpose is to gather as much information as possible before determining next steps (see Figure 5.9).

Here are some questions to consider answering during this step:

- Which questions had the highest degree of correct responses?
- Which questions were left blank?
- Are there any outliers or anomalies within the data?
- Which questions had the most incorrect responses?
- Are there any noticeable increases or decreases?

During this process, it is helpful to record group observations on chart paper. When the team begins the interpretation process, they can add another column to the chart. Keep in mind that the data being analyzed should be a reflection of the teachers' instructional effort and not just used for grading.

Data Discussion Step 2: Interpretation of the Data Being Analyzed

Once teams have identified what they see, it's time to infer what the data suggest. Achievement Teams help teachers and leaders make accurate inferences about the levels of mastery that students have achieved with respect to a specific learning target. During this discussion, the team looks at making several interpretations, with an emphasis of making sense of what the data reveal—and why. Teams are encouraged to think broadly with plenty of creativity (see Figure 5.9).

Here are some sample guiding questions:

- Based on these results, what are some criteria we might use to help us determine which is most important?
- What are some of our hunches about what might need to happen next?
- If we compare these results with data from previous assessments, can we show periods of improvement or decline?

FIGURE 5.9
Data Discussion Steps 1 and 2

Describing what we see before we form opinions	**Interpreting** assessment results and making inferences
• The team looks at data, taking turns describing what they see while holding off on any specific interpretations. • The focus is to discover trends, patterns, and common errors while also looking for results that indicate student understanding.	• Once teams have identified what they see, they begin to form opinions while trying to make sense of the data. • Team members form as many different interpretations as they can and begin to transition to root cause analysis.

Data Discussion Step 3: Implications for Classroom Practice

During this step, teams thoughtfully consider the highest-leverage instructional strategies and next steps to take back to their classrooms. Connecting back to interpretations, teams ask themselves, "What are the implications for classroom practice?"

- What are our next steps?
- What instructional strategies might be most effective?
- What types of assessments or activities can provide additional and accurate information?
- How can a conversation like this affect your own instruction and that of the entire team?

Create Relational Trust So Teams Can Operate at an Optimal Level

"When relational trust is strong, reform initiatives are more likely to be deeply engaged by school participants and to diffuse broadly across the organization" (Bryk & Schneider, 2002, p. 122). Relational trust and PLCs have a natural tendency to work well with each other, as trust can increase positive social exchanges. But what about teams that have limited trust? Researchers Bryk and Schneider (2002) spent 4 years in 12 Chicago school communities determining how the effects of relational trust influence school reform efforts. They developed a 5-point teacher trust scale to assist schools and districts with ascertaining the level of trust that exists among colleagues (ranging from "strongly disagree" to "strongly agree") with the following considerations:

- Teachers at this school trust one another.
- Teachers at this school feel comfortable discussing feelings, worries, and frustrations with other teachers.
- Teachers at this school respect other teachers who take the lead in improvement efforts.
- Teachers at this school respect other teachers who are experts at their craft.
- I feel respected by other teachers at this school. (Bryk & Schneider, 2002, p. 157)

Should you decide to administer this survey to your staff, Figure 5.10 includes a sample data set based on the survey results. The data collected uses a 5-point Likert scale. Each answer choice is coded from 1 = "strongly disagree" to 5 = "strongly agree." An advantage of this type of survey is that it can capture levels of agreement regarding a topic but in such a way that it does not force specific responses. In addition to collecting opinions, Likert scales measure the most frequent responses, which makes them easy to understand.

Based on these results, what are the implications for leading PLCs and teacher teams? How might leaders improve relational trust? Which responses from the survey cause the most concern? How might you prioritize these results? Would you share results with the people who participated in the survey? By measuring relational trust and devoting time to addressing trends, you begin the journey to minimizing the effects of mistrust in your school.

Leaders can and should broaden trust within a school organization. It is a key responsibility for leaders in education. Some of the more essential leadership attributes contributing to schoolwide relational trust are trustworthiness, respect, interdependence, empathy, ability, consistency, and integrity. Leaders who aim to build trust among their team members

FIGURE 5.10
Relational Trust Scale Sample Data

In this scenario, 50 educators were asked to complete the Relational Trust Survey (Bryk & Schneider, 2002). The data presented are not averages but a representation of the most frequent responses. The parenthetical number after each percentage is the raw score or number of respondents for each answer statement.

Number of Survey Respondents (N = 50)	1. Strongly Disagree	2. Disagree	3. Neutral	4. Agree	5. Strongly Agree
1. Teachers in this school trust one another.	16% (8)	38% (19)	20% (10)	14% (7)	12% (6)
2. Teachers at this school feel comfortable discussing feelings, worries, and frustrations with other teachers.	18% (9)	40% (20)	12% (6)	20% (10)	10% (5)
3. Teachers at this school respect other teachers who take the lead in school improvement efforts.	16% (8)	28% (14)	32% (16)	16% (8)	8% (4)
4. Teachers at this school respect other teachers who are experts at their craft.	22% (11)	12% (6)	34% (17)	18% (9)	14% (7)
5. I feel respected by other teachers at this school.	24% (12)	16% (8)	24% (12)	22% (11)	14% (7)

demonstrate active listening skills, especially when their colleagues express vulnerabilities. Fostering trust means leaders must recognize and address incompetence rather than allow it to persist. If you have ever been part of a work environment and noticed obvious negligence from leaders, then you are likely to question their ability to create an effective and stable environment. This requires leaders to address those moral or ethical issues that contradict your school's core values. By doing so, you heighten trust throughout the organization and demonstrate integrity.

What Bryk and Schneider (2002) discovered is that people can amplify relational trust through their social exchanges during collaboration. Even more notable are the regressive effects of an absence of trust, which results in schools having little or no chance of improving. Feeling trusted and respected can improve school reform efforts. Bryk and Schneider found that schools with substantial levels of trust at the outset of reforms have a one-in-two chance of making significant improvements in math and reading, whereas those with weak relationships have only a one-in-seven chance of making gains.

Lead Change in PLCs

Leaders who want to create special schools must do special things—and understand the difference between a *good* PLC and an *exceptional* PLC. Being a good PLC may not require much extra effort. It is likely that, if you are reading this book, you probably already have good PLCs. Exceptional PLCs, however, just hit different, and the difference between the two is obvious. When we lead change as it relates to collaboration, there is focused commitment between teachers and leaders based on drive and passion. As leaders, we must provide the tools necessary to facilitate innovative collaboration.

Figure 5.11 represents an introduction to innovative collaboration, where teams follow a consistent protocol designed to enhance instruction and achievement. Leading change means leading with clarity. We cannot expect teachers to become exceptional participants of high-functioning PLCs unless they are led with exceptional clarity.

One unfamiliar change I have supported instructional leaders in making is a cycle of pre-teaching and pre-assessment. Although this is atypical compared to traditional PLCs, this practice gives teachers more accurate and informative data. Leaders interested in focusing on the impact of PLCs should thoughtfully introduce this practice to their teachers, show them the evidence of why it works, and support them in implementing it. In Achievement Teams, teachers introduce a learning target to students before it is assessed, giving students adequate time to activate prior knowledge. This is called pre-teaching, so when students take assessments, they are not looking at skills they have never been taught. This means that the results from the pre-assessment are, in part, a reflection of the teacher's instructional

FIGURE 5.11
Teacher Team Essential Actions

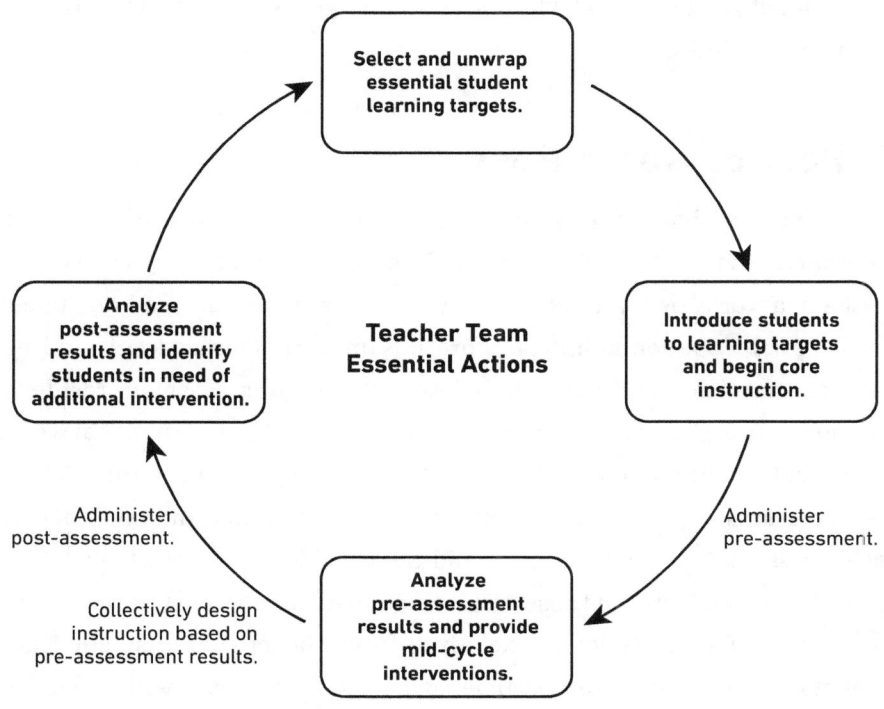

effort. This is an atypical cycle compared to traditional PLCs, but it can yield results that truly affect teaching and learning.

By pre-teaching and then pre-assessing, teachers receive data that can be more accurate and informative, which allows the teacher to connect the assessment to instruction. Once the first assessment is administered, teachers can use the analysis model explained earlier in this chapter. The graphic in Figure 5.12 suggests that teachers then collectively pool their best thoughts regarding instruction before the second assessment is administered. It is important to note that instruction between the pre- and post-assessment is not a repeat since it must address those gaps, mistakes, and misconceptions observed from the first assessment. Rather, it is an opportunity to create new learning that addresses specific errors. More important, when reteaching content that students struggle with, it's important to not reteach it the way you originally taught it. I have been providing professional development with this model for more than 10 years, and it has proven successful many times.

To Post or Not to Post

Many teachers have questioned the reason and purpose of the post-assessment and whether it's essential. Comments such as "This seems like a lot of extra work" or "I already know where my students are, so I don't need any more data" are common. Therefore, it is important for leaders to address these concerns by explaining that without the use of assessment results at the end of a pre/post cycle, we may miss an opportunity or a trend that would not be evident without data. First, a post-assessment measures growth from the pre-assessment and highlights students' strengths and weaknesses. Post-assessment results can also build the confidence of both teacher and students, especially when those results demonstrate marked improvement.

An option to consider is excluding from the post-assessment those students who demonstrated proficiency on the first assessment. Reassessment would be reserved for students who did not score at or higher than the proficient level. Figure 5.12 illustrates a visual model of this cycle that incorporates the use of a comprehensive assessment system while providing a continuum of research-based practices that are data-driven. This tiered approach using instruction and assessment can help support a wide range of learning needs within the general classroom setting. Additionally, leaders encouraging the use of this model can stress the importance of high-quality instruction that can provide targeted support for all students (universal) or for some students (supplemental).

Students who are not required to take the post-assessment would not necessarily move ahead with new content. Rather, they could increase their learning from deep to transfer by participating in learning that requires self-reflection, reciprocal teaching, and error analysis. Whether all students take the post-assessment or just those students who did not demonstrate

FIGURE 5.12
Pre- and Post-Assessment

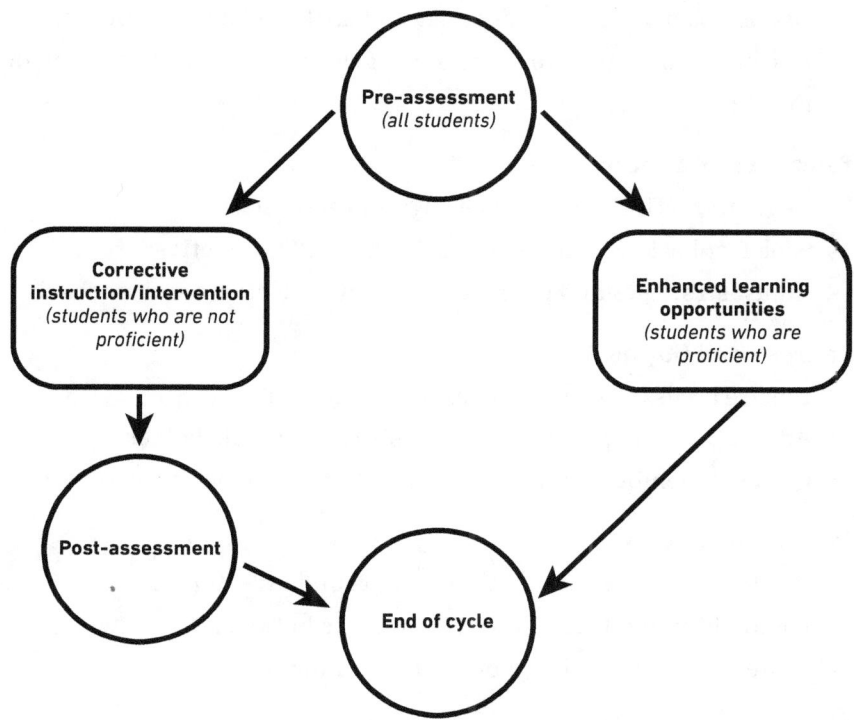

Source: Inspired by content from *Implementing Mastery Learning* (3rd ed.) (p. 21), by T. R. Guskey, 2023, Corwin.

proficiency on the first assessment, the importance of using data to promote a structured approach to instruction is sustainable and effective.

PLC Leadership Checklist

For leaders to effectively communicate and lead high-functioning, collaborative teams, there are certain conditions that must be present. On the surface, there is an obvious need to stress the importance of teacher collaboration and ensure deep, steadfast execution of the Achievement Teams process across all grade levels and departments. Creating a vision and purpose is the best place to start, but there are five deeper leadership traits to consider:

Data-Driven Discussions
- Analyze student data to inform instructional practices.
- Use assessments and other data to set goals and monitor progress.
- Encourage members to share strategies and resources based on data insights.

Reflection and Feedback
- Regularly reflect on PLC meetings and activities.
- Seek feedback from members to improve PLC effectiveness.
- Adjust strategies and practices based on reflections and feedback.

Resources and Support
- Ensure access to necessary resources and materials.
- Advocate for support from administration or stakeholders.
- Connect members with external resources or experts when needed.

Celebrate Successes
- Recognize and celebrate achievements and milestones.
- Highlight individual and collective contributions.
- Foster a positive and supportive environment.

Communication
- Maintain open and transparent communication with members.
- Share agendas, meeting minutes, and important updates regularly.
- Encourage two-way communication and active listening.

In concluding this chapter on the indicators of effective collaboration, I believe it is essential to recognize that the underlying principles of focused collaboration are not just theoretical ideals but practical necessities for educational success. The five profiles of collaboration—structuring successful teamwork, leveraging formative assessments, using data for informed decision making, fostering relational trust, and leading change—serve as pillars that uphold the dynamic process of continuous improvement in educational settings.

As educational leaders, embracing these profiles means committing to a culture in which collaboration transcends simple cooperation and becomes a transformative force. This commitment will not only enhance instructional practice but also foster an environment where both students and teachers thrive. By embedding these profiles into the fabric of daily interactions and decision-making processes within teacher teams, leaders can ensure that collaboration is not an occasional initiative but an ongoing pursuit of growth and educational excellence for all students.

"What? So What? Now What?" Critical Reflection Model

What? In this chapter, we explored four components that furthered our understanding of effective collaboration and key leadership moves to bring effective collaboration to life among the teams we work with:

1. The five leadership profiles that promote focused collaboration.
2. Reflection of our own facilitation of teacher collaboration and data analysis.
3. The four-step Achievement Teams protocol and the ways effective instructional leaders facilitate and participate in structured protocols.
4. Components of effective PLC leadership captured in a helpful checklist.

With a clearer vision of effective teacher collaboration and the leadership moves required to establish a collaborative culture, leaders are better equipped to implement and monitor systems and expectations that facilitate a collective commitment to ongoing improvement.

So What? What are the implications for this chapter and your leadership framework? What are the implications of the research?

_____

_____

_____

_____

Now What? What will you do differently as a result?

_____

_____

_____

_____

6

RESEARCH-DRIVEN MICROTEACHING AND LEARNING LABS

Introduction to Microteaching and Learning Labs

In this chapter, you'll learn how to combine microteaching and learning labs to further improve teacher collaboration across your school or district. Leaders can promote and support a powerful method that encourages teachers to experiment with instructional strategies that are unfamiliar or that require additional practice to develop confidence. However, microteaching and learning labs involve more than just practicing new instructional strategies. They also encourage innovation and provide an opportunity to incorporate action research where teachers investigate evidence-based practices that accelerate student achievement. This is a hands-on, experiential learning opportunity that combines the practical application of microteaching in a lablike setting.

Why is this chapter important? This chapter elaborates on the what, why, and how of two high-impact instructional coaching practices: microteaching and learning labs. It highlights proven success stories of schools that have implemented these practices so leaders can contextualize this "how-to" chapter in real classrooms.

How can it improve your personal leadership profile? Leaders who create and facilitate structures that enable deliberate practice and reflection, such as microteaching and learning labs, catalyze teacher performance such that instructional prowess significantly improves over shorter periods of time, spread best practices across classrooms in service of all students, and further solidify a culture of continuous learning among staff.

Microteaching in the Feedback Process

Microteaching, a research-based strategy with roots in teacher training programs, was first used to improve knowledge and understanding of instructional practice. As implied in the name, microteaching is a minilesson involving a small number of students. The lesson duration is relatively short, 10–20 minutes, and the demonstrating teacher practices an instructional strategy for subsequent evaluation. Originally designed for student teachers, microteaching is a self-reflection technique that includes the use of video.

Microteaching is now a common strategy in schools because of its effect on student learning and its ease of use for teachers and teams. When used effectively and deliberately, it can double the speed of learning (Hattie, 2009, 2012, 2023). It also simultaneously accelerates the practice of individual teachers and improves levels of collective teacher efficacy. The goal of microteaching is to combine the use of video and direct observation from peers. Hattie calculated an effect size for microteaching based on 426 studies involving 39,208 people (see Figure 6.1).

The confidence interval (or robustness) associated with this effect size is $R = 3$, based on a 1–5 scale, where 3 can be interpreted as "confident" in a particular finding. This means its use has a favorable probability of making a difference. An effect size of $d = 1.0$ indicates an increase of one standard

FIGURE 6.1
Microteaching Effect Size

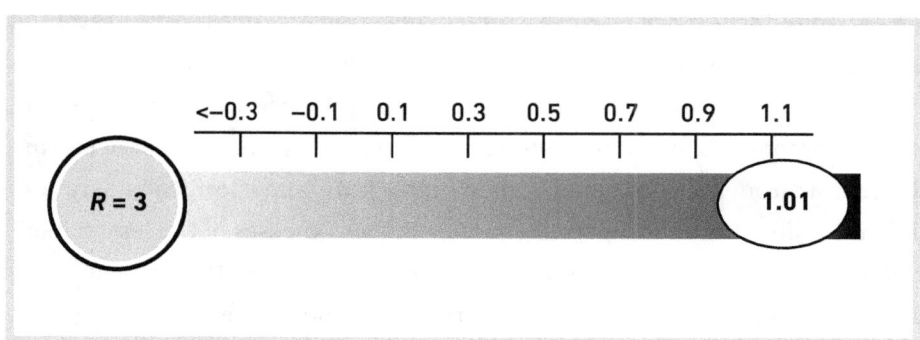

Source: Data from *Visible Learning: The Sequel,* by J. Hattie, 2023, Routledge. Copyright 2023 by John Hattie.

deviation on the outcome. In this case, the outcome is improving school achievement. A one-standard-deviation increase is typically associated with advancing students' achievement by two to three years, improving the rate of learning by 50 percent (Hattie, 2009). Therefore, the effect size of microteaching, $d = 1.01$, can be considered significant in terms of improving instruction.

When combined with feedback from peers, microteaching offers a valuable opportunity to improve practice for not only the teacher demonstrating the lesson but also others who can help refine the instruction and then use it across several classrooms. Jim Knight (2013) advocates for the use of video as a powerful tool to improve professional learning. "When we record ourselves doing our work, we see that reality is very different from what we think" (p. 2). Sometimes we're disappointed by what we see, but we're often delighted. Regardless, video helps us capture teacher and student behaviors we might otherwise overlook. Teachers can use video to improve their individual practice, but it's most powerful when used with colleagues and accompanied by dialogue and feedback.

Microteaching Cycle

Leaders and instructional coaches can create a microteaching cycle—and visualize the process—with a simple flowchart. It is important to understand that the demonstrating teacher may feel anxious or nervous as they model instruction. However, with multiple opportunities to practice, Murat Peker (2009) found that using microteaching in teaching practice reduces teaching anxiety level. The cycle I use incorporates the format shown in Figure 6.2.

This cycle gives teachers the opportunity to practice strategies and deliver lessons in a low-stakes environment, where the focus is not necessarily on how students performed, although this is an important consideration. It is more about evaluating the strengths and weaknesses of the lesson itself and how to make adjustments so all teachers can replicate the strategy being modeled. This type of teaching simulation scales down the entire lesson and permits both teachers and peers to begin the process of feedback.

Amobi and Irwin (2009) studied reflection statements from 31 secondary education teachers during a microteaching session and concluded that teachers felt that microteaching created a meaningful learning experience. Microteaching increases skill and knowledge acquisition ($d = 0.69$) while creating a comfortable environment by eliminating the need to have teachers practice a new instructional strategy in front of a large number of students. Leaders who wish to reap the benefits of microteaching can do three things:

1. Make time for microteaching (during already established PLC time).
2. Include microteaching as part of the professional plan for your school/district.
3. Organize microteaching opportunities by grade level and department.

Learning Labs

Learning labs are a form of microteaching that may include the use of video. As explained earlier, microteaching is a technique in which a teacher

FIGURE 6.2
Microteaching Cycle

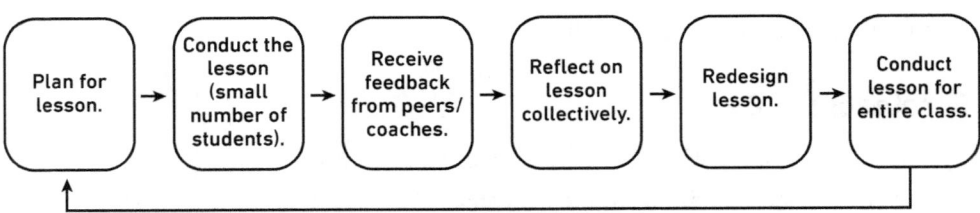

delivers a short lesson to a small number of students that is then analyzed by the teacher—or other teachers and leaders—for the purposes of improvement. In a learning lab, the teacher conducting the lesson is observed (not evaluated) by the rest of the grade- or content-level team. Observing teachers use a feedback form specific to the lesson being observed, and rather than record the lesson on video, the team delivers feedback in real time. After feedback has been delivered, the teacher modeling the instructional strategy reflects on how they felt about the delivery, how engaged the students were, and what they would do differently if given the opportunity to deliver the lesson again to an entire class.

This is perhaps the biggest advantage of learning labs: they provide an opportunity to receive feedback and reflect on practice. When leaders can create a hands-on environment in which teachers can learn new instructional techniques, they help increase collaboration, confidence, and, ultimately, student achievement. The combination of microteaching and learning labs forms a powerful partnership that results in multiple opportunities to learn new teaching methods. By providing support for targeted improvement, instructional coaches also play an important role in advancing instructional practices.

Setting Up Learning Labs

Learning labs can be conducted in various ways, depending on the school's specific goals, resources, and preferences. Here's a general overview of how schools might conduct them:

- **Planning and Preparation:** The school determines the objectives, content, and resources required for a learning lab, based on educational goals, students' needs, and curriculum requirements.
- **Curriculum Design:** Educators play a crucial role in developing the curriculum for the learning lab, tailoring it to their students' specific needs and interests. This process includes setting learning objectives, designing activities, and selecting resources.
- **Lab Setup:** The physical space for a learning lab might involve arranging desks or tables, setting up equipment or materials, and ensuring that the space is conducive to the planned activities.

- **Tools and Resources:** Educators choose the tools, resources, and materials needed for the lab activities. Resources could include textbooks, digital resources (e.g., educational websites, software applications), or other learning aids (e.g., interactive whiteboards, manipulatives).
- **Instruction and Facilitation:** Teachers or instructors lead the sessions, guiding students through the planned strategy, providing instruction, facilitating discussions, and offering support.
- **Hands-on Learning:** Learning labs often involve hands-on strategies that allow students to apply concepts learned in the classroom. This could include conducting experiments, solving problems, working on projects, or engaging in collaborative activities.
- **Group Work and Collaboration:** Depending on the activities, students may work individually or in groups. Collaborative learning is often encouraged since it promotes teamwork, communication skills, and critical thinking.
- **Feedback:** During the lab sessions, educators provide students with timely and specific feedback on their progress and understanding of the material.
- **Reflection and Review:** At the end of the lab, students are encouraged to reflect on their learning experiences and review key concepts or takeaways from the session. This practice reinforces learning and validates the educators' efforts, helping them recognize how their work is having a meaningful impact.
- **Follow-up and Extension:** Depending on the lab's outcomes, educators may plan follow-up activities or extensions to reinforce learning or explore related topics more deeply.

In order for learning labs to be successful, educators are required to take the following steps:

1. Encourage teachers from each grade level to choose an instructional strategy they would like to practice and get peer feedback on.
2. Ensure the strategy selected has the potential to make a significant impact. The Instructional Strategy Flipbook is a high-leverage resource for supporting intentional strategy selection. (See Chapter 3 for more information.) By familiarizing themselves with the flipbook, teachers

strengthen their toolkits with proven, content-blind strategies that work effectively for all students. Furthermore, the flipbook allows teams to choose among 25 strategies to use in a learning lab setting.
3. Have each teacher create a 15- to 20-minute engaging lesson they will model to a small group of four to six students.
4. Arrange for other teachers, coaches, and administrators to observe the lesson, record valuable information, and then provide feedback to the teacher modeling the lesson.
5. Schedule a peer feedback session after the lab is complete and students have returned to their classroom.
6. Encourage observers to share information they recorded on the feedback form. This feedback should include both commendations and recommendations.
7. After the feedback session, have all teachers on the same grade-level team design a plan to implement the strategy in their classrooms.

Learning Lab Feedback Form

The form in Figure 6.3 can be used to provide accurate feedback to teachers as they experiment with instructional strategies and learn from that experience. There are three domains for providing feedback:

1. Communicating with students (instruction)
2. Using questioning and discussion techniques
3. Using assessment in instruction

Each domain is accompanied with further explanations and "look-fors." The point of this feedback form is to highlight lesson observations, but observers should keep in mind that it is not necessary to look for and check off every category in each domain. There is additional space to record details about what teachers and students did during the lesson; this is a great place to make commendations and recommendations.

Feedback for Learning Lab Participants

Providing teachers with feedback after a learning lab is crucial for their professional development and improvement in teaching practices. Here's a structured approach you can follow to give effective feedback:

FIGURE 6.3
Learning Lab Feedback Form

Teacher Observing	Teacher Observation	What is the student doing?
Did the teacher explain what to do in the steps? **Domain 1: Communicating with Students** • Expectations for learning • Directions and procedures • Explanations of content • Use of oral and written language		
Did the teacher ask questions using academic vocabulary (e.g., part, whole)? **Domain 2: Using Questioning and Discussion Techniques** • Quality of responses • Discussion techniques • Student participation • Student engagement • Activities and assignments • Grouping of students • Instructional material and resources • Structure and pacing		
Did the teacher provide students with feedback? **Domain 3: Using Assessment in Instruction** • Assessment criteria • Monitoring of student learning • Feedback to students • Student self-assessment and monitoring of progress • Lesson adjustment		
Commendations:		
Recommendations:		

Note: Revised with permission from PS 249, The Caton School, Brooklyn, New York.

1. Start with positive feedback.
   - Begin by highlighting what went well during the lab.
   - Acknowledge the teacher's strengths, efforts, and achievements.
   - Use positive reinforcement to boost confidence and create a receptive environment for constructive feedback.
2. Be specific.
   - Provide specific examples of what you observed during the lab.
   - Instead of general statements like "Good job," say something like, "I noticed how you engaged all students by using different questioning techniques."
3. Focus on areas of improvement.
   - Address areas where the teacher could improve or try different strategies.
   - Frame suggestions as opportunities for growth rather than criticism.
   - Offer suggestions with phrases such as "Have you considered . . ." or "You might try . . . ."
4. Use a constructive tone.
   - Ensure your feedback is delivered in a positive and supportive manner.
   - Avoid using negative language or making the teacher feel defensive.
   - Be respectful and empathetic in your communication.
5. Encourage reflection and self-assessment.
   - Encourage the teacher to reflect on their own performance during the learning lab.
   - Ask open-ended questions to stimulate self-assessment, such as "How do you think that activity engaged the students?" or "What might you do differently next time?"
6. Provide resources or additional support.
   - Offer resources, materials, or training opportunities that can help the teacher improve in specific areas.
   - Provide opportunities for the teacher to observe other experienced educators or participate in professional development workshops.

Remember, the goal of providing feedback after a learning lab is to support the teacher's growth and improvement. By offering specific, constructive, and supportive feedback, you help teachers enhance their teaching practices and ultimately benefit their students' learning experiences.

Learning Labs in Action: A Title I School's Success with Microteaching

PS 249, The Caton School, is located in Brooklyn, New York. The school has exponentially elevated teacher clarity and performance in a high-poverty elementary school, bridging the typical performance gap between novice and seasoned educators.

The transformative impact of Achievement Teams at PS 249 is evident. Some key outcomes include

- **Excellence in Student Academic Achievement:** The Caton School was the top math performer in their district in the 2022–23 school year, with 76 percent of students proficient or higher, an increase of 15 percentage points over the year before. In 2021, several years into Achievement Teams and lab site work, The Caton School received a Blue Ribbon Award for Exemplary Performance from the U.S. Department of Education. In 2023, the school earned an America's Best School Award from the National Center for Urban School Transformation.
- **Achievement Teams Implementation:** PS 249 was named a Reward School for two years in a row (2018–19) for high academic achievement—with no significant gaps between subgroups—by the New York Department of Education. Not only are multilingual students thriving academically, they are also reaching fluency and moving into regular classrooms at a much higher rate than before.
- **Consistent and Effective Data Analysis Across Grade Levels and Classrooms:** The structured approach to data analysis and instructional planning continues to contribute to sustained academic excellence.
- **An Innovative Lab Site Work Model That Ensures Deliberate Practice:** Lab sites emerged as a linchpin for teacher professional development, offering immediate feedback and a safe space for practice.

 Read the entire case study here (https://www.steveventura.com/wp-content/uploads/2024/10/ACS-Case-Study-PS249v2.pdf) and learn more about how this exceptional school has built coherence throughout the entire building.

"What? So What? Now What?" Critical Reflection Model

What? The main objective of microteaching, as stated by Otsupius (2014), is that it enables teachers to learn and assimilate new teaching skills under controlled conditions. By getting granular about best practices, leaders are equipped to accelerate instructional improvement and student growth with this high-impact strategy. In this chapter, we explored the ins and outs of microteaching and learning labs, including

1. What microteaching and learning labs are.
2. The microteaching cycle.
3. Steps for setting up learning labs.
4. Ways to maximize feedback cycles during learning labs.
5. Ways to leverage the Instructional Strategy Flipbook during microteaching and learning labs.

So What? What are the implications for this chapter and your leadership framework? What are the implications of the research?

_____
_____
_____
_____

Now What? What will you do differently as a result?

_____
_____
_____
_____

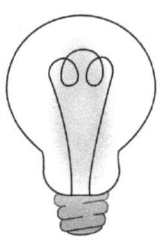

7

USING ARTIFICIAL INTELLIGENCE TO ENHANCE TEACHER TEAMS

Before we begin exploring the function of artificial intelligence (AI) in education, we need to define this technology in its most basic form. The *Oxford English Dictionary* defines AI as "the theory and development of computer systems able to perform tasks that normally require human intelligence, such as visual perception, speech recognition, decision making, and translation between languages." In 1950, English mathematician Alan Turing introduced a test to determine if a machine is capable of thinking. An interrogator asks questions to both a computer program and a human being, with both being secluded from the interrogator. Based on the responses, the interrogator must then determine if the answers provided were generated by the human participant or the machine. If the interrogator is unable to distinguish between the two, then the computer has acquired "artificial intelligence."

AI has changed drastically since then, and it now includes countless ways that educators can incorporate the technology into their work. Educators, like the wider public, experience a range of emotions about this topic. Some readily embrace AI, whereas some would prefer to ban its use altogether. Moreover, many educators feel that when students use AI to correct their grammar and spelling, among other things, they are denied the opportunity to develop their own fundamental learning skills. Academic dishonesty sits at the top of most teachers' concerns, since AI tools, such as ChatGPT, can generate papers, reports, and projects in a matter of seconds.

Why is this chapter important? Leaders must be willing to explore the implications of emerging technologies such as artificial intelligence and make important decisions about its application and use. The use of AI is not intended to replace teachers. By contrast, its use can maximize teacher collaboration and free up precious time and energy for educators to focus on providing students with excellent instruction. "Ultimately, AI has the potential to redefine education by creating entirely new methods of learning and collaboration, propelled by its data-driven insights and adaptive capabilities" (Lang-Raad, 2025, p. 5).

How can it improve your personal leadership profile? When leaders are knowledgeable in their use of relevant technology, they build credibility with both teachers and students. Through thoughtful and responsible application of AI, leaders can streamline systems and reallocate time and resources accordingly.

This chapter focuses on how AI can improve collaborative protocols. At this moment, educators are observing an incredible technological revolution where AI has an ever-increasing presence. For example, ChatGPT Edu was introduced in May 2024 and will be referred to in this chapter as an important tool for educators.

By design, this chapter does not address various student applications for AI, as this is an ever-changing landscape and not connected to the core goal of this book, which is to equip instructional leaders with the tools, structures, and strategies necessary to unlock meaningful academic growth within their schools. However, there are several student-centered

AI-driven learning activities that don't give direct answers, complete work for students, or guide student learning by replacing their effort. Don't be intimidated by AI and instead learn how you can leverage its capabilities to increase student learning.

I have always considered myself a competent consumer of technology and frequently ponder how I could use it to enhance my personal and professional life. As I looked for AI applications to enhance teacher collaboration, I discovered that there are more than I had imagined. Therefore, I have narrowed my focus on the use of AI specific to the Achievement Teams process.

The Achievement Teams Four-Step Meeting Protocol: A Refresher

Before we dig into applications of AI for each of the four steps in the Achievement Teams protocol, let's review the protocol itself. Achievement Teams use a four-step meeting protocol with a continuous cycle (Ventura & Ventura, 2022). Here's a brief overview:

- **Step 1: Collect and chart the data.** Achievement Teams focus on evidence from high-quality short-cycle assessments.
- **Step 2: Set SMART goals.** Based on short-cycle assessment data, Achievement Teams co-create SMART goals. Creating goals for both students and teachers has a tremendous effect on academic outcomes.
- **Step 3: Create baseline evidence statements.** Achievement Teams craft baseline evidence statements. By summarizing collected data, educators make inferences about students' mastery levels.
- **Step 4: Select high-yield instructional strategies.** Teachers select the strategies that will have the greatest effect on student achievement.

Now let's explore how an AI tool, such as ChatGPT, can assist with each of these steps, complete with examples and recommendations. As with any use of AI, users must be clear about how they intend to use AI and what limitations there may be. For example, although it is entirely possible to enter students' raw scores from assessments and get tables or spreadsheets in return, at the time of writing, ChatGPT cannot create pie charts, bar charts, or scatter plots. To bridge this gap, teachers can export AI-analyzed data into platforms such as Google Sheets or Microsoft Excel, where they can easily create custom visuals to support data-driven instruction. Ultimately, you need to consider how the tools you use can enhance and supplement the work you do while keeping in mind the important role that only you, the teacher, can fulfill.

Creating Short-Cycle Assessments Using AI

Short-cycle assessments can mean different things, so I want to be clear about how to use them in conjunction with Achievement Teams. Short-cycle assessments are pre- and post-assessments that teachers administer anywhere from two to four weeks apart. Teachers often administer them before ending a unit of instruction, and they typically do not grade them due to their formative purpose. The assessments provide initial baseline information teachers can use to inform instructional planning for both individual students and an entire class. Further, they provide feedback about instructional success and enable teachers to answer these four focus questions:

1. What strengths and gaps do the assessment results show?
2. What skills (verbs) and concepts (nouns and noun phrases) were achieved from the learning target, and what still needs to be learned?
3. Who did we teach effectively, and who still needs help?
4. Which instructional strategies were effective? Which ones were less effective?

Using AI to create these assessments can be extremely effective, assuming that the information is formatted and submitted to deliver optimal results. Let's dig into an example. Here is a sample generation prompt used to create an assessment for 7th grade English language arts:

> Please generate four multiple-choice questions and one short answer question for a 7th grade informational text assessment. Cite several pieces of textual evidence to support analysis of what the text says explicitly as well as inferences drawn from the text. Each question should have one correct answer and three incorrect plausible options. Include the answer key.

This simple prompt created an assessment in a matter of seconds. Teachers can refine the prompt to modify distractors, include multiple-choice questions with more than one answer, and add a post-assessment that evaluates the same skills:

Question 1: Which of the following best demonstrates a strong use of textual evidence to support an inference?

A) Stating a personal opinion about the text without citing any examples
B) Quoting a single word from the text without explaining its significance
C) Providing multiple quotes from the text and explaining how they support the inference
D) Summarizing the entire passage without referring to specific details

Answer: C

Question 2: A student reads an article about climate change and writes, "The author believes that human activity is the main cause of global warming." What should the student do to support this claim with textual evidence?

A) Restate the claim in their own words to make it more persuasive.
B) Find and cite multiple statements from the text that show the author's stance.
C) Ignore the text and focus on their personal beliefs about climate change.
D) Use a quote from a different article to provide supporting evidence.

Answer: B

Question 3: In an informational text about space exploration, the author states, "NASA's new Mars rover is designed to search for signs of ancient life." What inference can be made based on this statement?

A) The Mars rover is looking for living creatures on Mars today.
B) Scientists believe there may have been life on Mars in the past.
C) NASA does not believe that Mars ever had water.
D) The rover will only be collecting rock samples, not analyzing them.

Answer: B

Question 4: Which of the following statements best explains why citing multiple pieces of evidence is important in a text analysis?

A) It allows the reader to form their own opinion without relying on the text.
B) It makes the analysis longer, which improves the overall writing.
C) It strengthens the argument by showing different points that support the claim.
D) It helps the writer avoid using direct quotes from the text.

Answer: C

Question 5: Read the following excerpt from an article about space exploration:

> "NASA's newest Mars rover is equipped with advanced technology designed to analyze soil samples for signs of ancient microbial life. Scientists believe that if evidence of past life exists on Mars, it will likely be found in the layers of rock that have preserved the planet's history."

What inference can be made about the purpose of the Mars rover?

To ensure the validity and reliability of any AI-generated short-cycle assessment, a teacher should vet the assessment and ensure it is appropriate for the content being assessed. I cannot stress enough the importance of this step. Remember, AI is still prone to errors, so it is good practice to double-check all AI-generated results.

Step 1: Collect and Chart the Data Using AI

Once a pre-assessment is created and administered to students, it's time to engage in Step 1 of the Achievement Teams protocol: collect and chart the data. Let's examine some ways that AI can support this step. Let's say the pre-assessment was administered to 20 students and results were scored. Achievement Teams use four performance levels and cut scores. Figure 7.1 shows a breakdown of the number of students in each performance band. This is a very simple frequency distribution, where Excelling = number of students who answered all five questions correctly, Achieving = number

FIGURE 7.1
AI-Generated Student Assessment Results Chart

Performance Level	Number of Students	Percentage	Average Score
Excelling	5	25%	95
Achieving	1	5%	85
Progressing	8	40%	70
Beginning	6	30%	55
Total	20	100%	72.25

of students who answered four of the five questions correctly, Progressing = number of students who answered three of the five questions correctly, and Beginning = number of students who answered two or fewer of the five answers correctly.

This table was produced from the following prompt:

> Please organize these data into a table, including the overall average score of the assessment: 5 students who are Excelling, 1 student who is Achieving, 8 students who are Progressing, and 6 students who are Beginning.

Although the chart in Figure 7.1 is somewhat simple, it demonstrates how AI can quickly organize assessment results into a table, allowing teachers to clearly see the number and percentage of students in each performance area and the overall average. This structured format saves precious time, quickly organizes information, and provides clarity with a visual representation. As a reminder, the data gathered from a pre-assessment *should not be graded*. I requested the class average in this example, but I would not share this information with students. The use of averaging is an extremely emotional topic, and the average often does not accurately reflect student learning. It should, however, be used to determine intervention strategies and organize group scores.

It's worth pointing out that I have created a data collection form that can create basic tables, available via this QR code (bit.ly/ATspreadsheet). This resource helps you accurately reflect and communicate specific information about teachers and their students. Visual representation is an essential  consideration. For example, teachers can enter assessment results, goals, and instructional strategies. Likewise, leaders can organize pre- and post-assessment results by teacher groups or individual teachers.

Step 2: Set SMART Goals Using AI

After collecting and charting assessment data, we move on to Step 2 of the Achievement Teams protocol—setting SMART goals—which AI tools can also support. Goal setting is a critical part of the Achievement Teams meeting protocol, as goals create motivation for both teachers and students. Based on my time in classrooms across the country, I've witnessed far too many frequently missed opportunities for teachers and students to communicate the specific goals of a lesson. Goals must be moderately challenging, especially when we use them in a collaborative process. Hattie (2009) believes that "goals have a self-energizing effect if they are appropriately challenging for the student, as they can motivate students to exert effort in line with the difficulty or demands of the goal" (p. 164).

In Achievement Teams, SMART goals are used to create a growth target between the pre- and post-assessments. Achievement Teams follow the SMART goal framework formulated by George T. Doran (1981), which stipulates that goals should be specific, measurable, achievable, relevant, and time-bound. Continuing with our 7th grade informational text example, here is a sample generation prompt used to create SMART goals based on pre-assessment data:

> Please create a SMART goal example based on a pre- and post-assessment cycle for 7th grade. Cite several pieces of textual evidence to support analysis of what the text says explicitly as well as inferences drawn from the text.

The results from this prompt are as follows:

> **Specific:** Improve the student's ability to cite several pieces of textual evidence to support both explicit and inferential analysis of informational texts. Instruction will focus on identifying direct textual evidence, making logical inferences, and explaining how evidence supports their analysis.
>
> **Measurable:** Increase the class average score on the reading for informational text assessment questions from 40% on the pre-assessment to 75% on the post-assessment, with particular focus on students' ability to integrate multiple pieces of evidence effectively.
>
> **Achievable:** This goal will be accomplished through structured instructional strategies, including close reading, guided annotation, sentence frames for citing evidence, small-group discussions, and peer feedback activities. Students who need additional support will receive targeted assistance through small-group instruction and scaffolded graphic organizers.

Relevant: Mastering the ability to cite and explain textual evidence is a critical college and career readiness skill that enhances comprehension across all subject areas. This standard also builds essential analytical skills needed for success in higher-level reading and writing tasks.

Time-bound: Students will achieve this goal within four weeks, culminating in a post-assessment at the end of the instructional cycle.

Summary: Students will improve their ability to cite and analyze textual evidence, increasing their assessment score from 40% to 72% within four weeks. This will be achieved through targeted instruction, structured practice, and scaffolded supports, ensuring students can confidently identify, cite, and explain multiple pieces of textual evidence in informational texts.

These results are a good representation of a SMART goal. In reality, it may contain too much information, especially if we want to share this goal with students. However, I used additional information to refine the AI goal. Specifically, I added the following details:

The percentage of 7th grade students scoring proficient or higher using a reading informational text assessment will increase from 40 percent to 72 percent by the end of February 19 as measured by a team-created, formative short-cycle assessment administered on February 18.

After some tweaks, the refined SMART goal narrows in on the necessary information and is brief enough to share with students:

Specific: We are focusing on a single learning target.

Measurable: We will calculate growth between pre- and post-assessment results (40% to 72%).

Achievable: Our goal is set at an appropriate level of challenge.

Relevant: Students struggle with this learning target. If they master it, they will enter the next grade level with confidence and a readiness to learn.

Time-bound: We have set a date to determine progress and growth.

Step 3: Create Baseline Evidence Statements Using AI

With SMART goals in hand, we can use AI to create baseline evidence statements, which are statements that summarize the evidence that teams have gathered from the administration of a short-cycle pre-assessment. Using the data gathered during Step 1, we can use AI to develop a pathway for instructional strategy selection. Baseline evidence statements are also referred to as root cause analysis, where teams make inferences regarding student progress by analyzing pre-assessment results. Often, these statements help identify student needs and ultimately inform teachers where specific instructional strategies can address those needs.

The following prompt is based on the assessment results collected during Step 1, which simulate the areas where students were successful and where they needed additional support:

> Please identify the strengths and gaps from the results of the informational text pre- and post-assessments.

The results from this prompt are as follows:

Strengths:

Improvement Over Time: The student's score improved from 40% on the pre-assessment to 70% on the post-assessment, indicating a solid understanding of the material by the end of the learning cycle.

Understanding of Key Concepts: The increased accuracy in identifying explicit textual evidence and making logical inferences supported by multiple pieces of evidence. This suggests an improved understanding of how to analyze informational texts effectively.

Effective Learning Strategies: The use of structured reading strategies, close reading activities, guided annotation, and scaffolded sentence frames contributed to student progress. Small-group discussions and peer feedback activities reinforced comprehension and evidence-based responses.

Gaps:

Initial Knowledge Deficit: The pre-assessment score of 40% indicates that many students, particularly those in the Beginning and Progressing levels, struggled with distinguishing explicit details from inferred meaning and citing multiple pieces of evidence to support their responses.

Remaining Areas for Improvement: Despite the improvement, a 70% score on the post-assessment suggests that some students still struggle with explaining how their cited evidence supports their analysis. Students may need additional practice in integrating evidence smoothly into their responses.

Specific Content Gaps: If the post-assessment results show that students struggled with higher-order thinking questions, such as making inferences based on subtle textual clues, this highlights an area for targeted intervention. Additional instruction on evaluating the strength and relevance of evidence may also be needed.

As you can see, the AI tool created a summary of strengths and gaps, providing initial insights that can propel teams to go deeper, which in turn promotes rigorous levels of collaborative discourse. Remember, the data we collect and analyze are only as good as the assessments we use. Valid and reliable assessment results create opportunities for challenging conversations. If the data we collect do not challenge us, they will not change us.

Step 4: Select High-Yield Instructional Strategies Using AI

We have now arrived at the final step of the Achievement Teams protocol, where teachers select the strategies that will have the greatest effect on student achievement. The first three steps helped with data analysis, goal setting, and root cause analysis, so the instructional strategies teachers choose in this step must align with the results of those steps. Here, once again, we can use AI to address student misunderstandings and misconceptions—or the gaps that were identified in Step 3:

What instructional strategies can teachers explore to address the gaps identified in the previous step?

The results from this prompt are as follows:

Targeted Small-Group Sessions: Group students based on their specific needs and gaps identified in the assessments. Provide targeted instruction on distinguishing explicit details from inferences, citing multiple pieces of evidence, and explaining how evidence supports their claims. Use scaffolded questioning to guide students through analysis.

Interactive Text Annotation: Teach students to use annotation strategies such as Mark It Up. Have them highlight explicit evidence, underline implicit details, and add margin notes explaining their reasoning. This will help students actively engage with the text and track evidence for their responses.

Guided Practice: Begin with teacher-led modeling of Claim-Evidence-Reasoning (CER) writing, demonstrating how to structure responses with multiple pieces of textual evidence. Gradually release responsibility to students through peer discussions and independent writing activities.

Cooperative Group Activities: Implement a Jigsaw text analysis, where small groups of students analyze different sections of a text to identify central claims and supporting evidence. Groups then come together to share findings and build a comprehensive understanding of how textual evidence supports analysis.

Digital Tools for Writing Support: Utilize AI-powered tools such as ChatGPT, Google Docs AI, or Quill.org to help students refine their citation and analysis. These tools can provide sentence starters, suggest stronger wording, and guide students in structuring evidence-based responses.

Exit Tickets for Formative Assessment: At the end of each lesson, have students complete a two-column exit ticket where they write two pieces of evidence from the day's reading and explain how each one supports their analysis. This will provide quick insight into student progress and areas needing reinforcement.

Reflections on the Need for Ethical and Responsible AI Use in Education

As leaders, it is essential that we recognize the many legitimate concerns people have about the use of AI in education. It is equally important that we consider and address those concerns with teams before introducing specific AI tools, especially during collaborative team cycles. There are educators who have grave concerns about the use of AI. Some fear it can reduce teachers' capacity, influence job security, or replace them altogether. Some worry about decreased human capital and social interaction. Others simply do not have any knowledge about what AI is and how they can incorporate it into an educational setting. I believe leaders can assist teachers in the use of AI by stressing how it can elevate teaching and learning, emphasizing that the focus should be less on the tools and more on improving teaching practices.

Professional learning opportunities specific to the use of AI are a must for all teachers. That said, leaders should downplay the idea that AI can simply create an assessment or a unit of study. Teachers must know that *all* AI-generated content must be used as a foundation to further the use of sound instructional practices, such as transfer strategies, teacher clarity, and scaffolding.

When used intentionally and thoughtfully, AI can support teacher teams that are based on an established initiative, such as PLCs or Achievement Teams. Leaders should therefore encourage the use of AI by giving teachers the opportunity to take risks, innovate, and experiment with AI tools to improve the quality of their teaching.

Finally, my recommendation on using AI within the context of teacher collaboration is to first get PLCs up and running, ensuring there is a clear understanding of the purpose and meaning of collaborative team cycles—which is to improve instructional practice. Then, when teams have mastered the protocol for effective PLCs, strategically introducing AI would be better received because teachers can then realize the potential these tools have to improve current school initiatives.

Once foundational practices such as PLCs and collaborative cycles are established, schools can begin shaping AI policies that empower teachers and protect instructional integrity. Educators play a crucial role in this process, making them feel empowered and integral. Begin by clearly defining acceptable uses of AI tools—for example, allowing AI for brainstorming or drafting but not for completing final assessments. Encourage transparency by having students acknowledge when and how AI tools were used in their work. Establish guardrails that promote ethical use, such as emphasizing original thinking, citing AI-generated content when appropriate, and incorporating teacher check-ins or revision checkpoints. A well-crafted policy should support responsible exploration of AI while reinforcing critical thinking, authorship, and accountability.

"What? So What? Now What?" Critical Reflection Model

What? In this chapter, we examined ways that AI tools and carefully crafted prompts can support and enhance teacher collaboration. We

1. Explored AI tools and corresponding prompts to support each of the four steps in the Achievement Teams protocol.
2. Studied AI responses to prompts aligned with the four-step Achievement Teams protocol.
3. Considered how to responsibly incorporate emerging technologies, such as AI, into our work as educators.

By demonstrating openness and thoughtfulness around the incorporation of AI tools into daily leadership and instructional practices, leaders model a continuous learning disposition. When placing emphasis on AI tools' ability to streamline workflows and free up precious teacher time, leaders communicate their care for educators' workloads and help them create a healthier work-life balance.

So What? What are the implications for this chapter and your leadership framework? What are the implications of the research?

_____
_____
_____
_____

Now What? What will you do differently as a result?

_____
_____
_____
_____

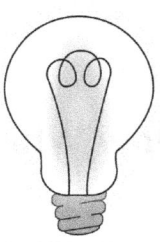

8

PUTTING IT ALL TOGETHER

Let's synthesize the previous chapters to make important connections that can inform your leadership work moving forward. This chapter encourages you to consider your leadership tendencies and the dispositions that affect your ability to enact change. When paired with strong instructional leadership and a focus on effective collaboration, leaders who hone their self-reflection and are committed to continuous growth can foster the organizational culture necessary for all students to succeed.

Why is this chapter important? Leaders who embrace collaboration as a cornerstone to improve academic achievement cannot simply hope their actions will work. The intentional actions included here ensure that success is within reach, as long as leaders are willing to create a clear and specific vision and then monitor outcomes accordingly.

How can it improve your personal leadership profile? Effective school leadership must be created by design. The best leaders possess several common traits, such as integrity, consistency, and empathy. Furthermore, empathetic leaders understand that decision making—a trait associated with confidence and competence—is shared.

Collective Leadership Pre- and Post-Reflection

When we started exploring ways to effectively lead the collective, we self-assessed our beliefs about our leadership skills, along with our perceptions of what makes a strong leader. Review the leadership beliefs in Figure 8.1 and indicate whether you agree or disagree with each statement in the After column. After this reflection, revisit the anticipation guide and your initial reflections in Figure 1.1 on page 6. Compare your responses to see if they changed.

Leadership Vision and Culture

Informed leaders can truthfully reflect on the impact they have. Of course, leaders want to encourage autonomy, trust, and creativity, all of which go hand in hand with effective instructional leadership. But how is this accomplished? In short, through culture and the willingness to lead.

The culture you create is the culture you deserve. If you have ever been part of a flourishing school or school district, you know that a forward-thinking leader often wields the influence and power to create a healthy culture based on shared values, a shared vision, and meaningful relationships. These characteristics are what fuel many of today's most successful schools and districts. In previous chapters, I shared specific examples and strategies that improve collaboration and student success. However, without a clear leadership vision, especially one that stresses the importance of a culture that emphasizes relationships and trust, I am afraid many of these strategies won't bring about the intended impact.

A study of 12 instructionally effective school districts in California analyzed the organizational structures that foster overall improvement (Murphy & Hallinger, 1988). The results were based on superintendent interviews, characteristics of the curriculum, and methods used by central offices to coordinate work activities in each school. Ultimately, the study uncovered three notable and distinctive themes associated with all 12 districts:

- **Labor Peace:** Across all 12 districts, it was apparent that there were no serious problems or issues between teachers and administration.

FIGURE 8.1
Anticipation Guide

Directions: Respond to each item with Agree or Disagree in the After column.

Before		Beliefs	After	
Agree	Disagree		Agree	Disagree
		Effective leaders encourage competition with others in the school or district.		
		Leaders can choose the way they want to use their time by prioritizing what needs to be accomplished.		
		Effective leaders adapt their leadership by adjusting different approaches for different situations.		
		Instructional leaders are keenly aware of the instructional practices being incorporated in their buildings.		
		Instructional coaches can increase positive teacher emotions by creating a no-fault reflection process where teachers can learn from mistakes.		
		Instructional coaches should facilitate PLCs and achievement teams.		
		Artificial intelligence can reduce critical thinking and is difficult to integrate with collaboration.		
		Instructional leaders should avoid observing classrooms where they may not have content expertise.		

Which of your opinions remained the same from the beginning to the end of this book? Which opinions changed? What reflections or lessons influenced your shift in opinion?

_____

_____

_____

_____

Additionally, the school boards were characterized as noninterfering and supportive. In fact, all the boards were actively involved in forming the direction of the district, which increased community acceptance. This finding suggests that when people are happy, they are also more productive.

- **Focus on Productivity and Improvement:** With a positive culture and atmosphere of cooperation, all 12 districts were able to keep their eyes squarely on increasing student proficiency levels. There was no real limit in terms of accomplishing this task, as there were no observable factors indicating that increased achievement could not be attained. In fact, not only were these districts found to be productivity focused, but they were also dedicated to improvement through goal-setting. In addition, they were careful not to overly invest in new programs. Data collection and analysis supported this laserlike focus on improvement and were used to make informed decisions about teaching, learning, and leadership. Strong instructional leadership at the superintendent level ensured consistency of instructional activities and played an essential role in improving the culture.

- **Organizational Dynamics:** This finding was somewhat complex because there was a healthy dose of district control across the school sites. However, at the same time, the superintendents of these districts spoke of the autonomy and flexibility they readily allowed and encouraged. This balance between control and autonomy seems to indicate something called "responsible autonomy," which was coined by sociologist Erik Trist (Trist & Murray, 1990). As the term suggests, it is possible to encourage autonomy and employee discretion while staying within specific parameters. By contrast, autonomy in this context does not mean doing anything one would like to do.

The superintendents of all 12 districts stressed that, even though there were certain areas of control, each principal and school had autonomy over the work they were tasked to complete with accountability to the district goals. One final and apparent observation was that a large part of their collective success was attributed to a finding that is consistent with many different leadership studies: *The leaders in these schools were seen doing what they required others to do.*

✏️ **Self-Assessment**

If you were to compare your current school or district to the three characteristics previously listed, where might you assess your own current reality? Remember, self-assessment and reflection are a cornerstone of today's most successful leaders, especially for those who emphasize the importance of ongoing improvement and adaptation.

_____

_____

_____

_____

_____

Developing and Implementing a Shared Vision

The implementation of Achievement Teams and PLCs requires leaders to organize school teams that relentlessly pursue effective collaboration. This can be difficult work, but competent leaders are able to establish a vision by focusing on creating a safe, equitable learning environment for all. Like any other high-impact initiative, leaders must lead from the front. They must also be equipped to identify what is missing from strategic initiatives and decide how to execute a successful launch. Complex change requires leaders to clearly and effectively communicate those components across stakeholder groups.

The Lippitt-Knoster Model is a leadership tool designed to help leaders manage complex change (see Figure 8.2, p. 129). Developed by psychologist Ronald Lippitt and educational expert Timothy Knoster, this visual model outlines explicit components that promote successful change (Caredda, 2020). The modified version I created is designed specifically for Achievement Teams and PLCs and serves as a road map for change implementation through the collective power of highly efficacious teams. My adaptation includes five components and stresses the consequences that may occur when a component is missing:

1. **Action Plan:** Action plans for stronger and more meaningful levels of collaboration are essential. They can include creating a formal feedback system, providing technical support for teaching, learning from facilitators or instructional coaches, and identifying instructional and assessment resources that currently align with Achievement Teams. Action plans can also help schools and districts start something right away, which is crucial because school systems are more likely to implement changes if they do so within 100 days from when they adopt those changes. Without an action plan, teams experience a false start, leading to low or no momentum and abandoning otherwise worthwhile initiatives.

2. **Collective Efficacy:** Collective efficacy includes "the perceptions of teachers in a school that the faculty as a whole can organize and execute the courses of action required to have a positive effect on students" (Goddard, 2002, p. 100). Leaders maximize collective efficacy by sharing master and vicarious experiences. As Mike Schmoker (1999) notes, "Collaboration allows teachers to capture each other's fund of collective intelligence" (p. 100). Without collective efficacy, there are fragmented and inconsistent beliefs across a team, undermining optimism in teamwide efforts.

3. **Goals:** Goals have a self-energizing effect and can motivate teams to exert effort in line with a specific task. This points to the importance of setting short-term goals that lead to long-term success. Goals set over shorter periods of time motivate, create focus, and increase the possibility of success. Without goals, teams have no way of measuring or noting improvement, which takes a major hit on organizational motivation.

4. **Formative Evaluation:** In addition to the use of assessment, formative evaluation is more about the interpretations of teachers' success and less about testing. As Hattie (2009) suggests, it's not only about the use of formative assessment but also about additional methods teachers can use to interpret the quality of learning. Without

formative evaluation, teams lack the evidence they need to stay the course or adjust in pursuit of improvement.
5. **Instructional Leadership:** Today's instructional leaders must be evaluators. They must routinely assess the effects they and their colleagues have on student learning, question what they need to improve, and decide on the evidence they need to do this work. Without strong instructional leadership, teams are left feeling confused—an utterly frustrating experience for hardworking educators.

Each of these five components must be present in order to achieve effective change. If any one component is missing, it can be interpreted in this manner:

- No action plan = False start
- No collective efficacy = Fragmented beliefs
- No goals = Reduced motivation
- No formative evaluation = Lack of evidence
- No instructional leadership = Confusion

When teams overcome barriers, leaders can realize the advantages of coordinated and intentional collaboration. The advantage of this simple yet important framework is that it helps leaders break down some of the more complex elements that comprise school improvement, with an emphasis on collaboration. It can assist with exposing and addressing identified gaps with explicit and shared leadership strategies, such as autonomy, empowerment, and accountability (WalkMe Team, 2024).

Leading with Empathy

Empathetic leadership means having the ability to understand the needs of others and being aware of other people's feelings and thoughts. Being an educational leader is not an easy task, as it requires a mix of several different, and at times competing, abilities or competencies. However, empathy is a skill that can have a positive effect on employee well-being (Gentry, 2024).

It's important to remember the difference between sympathy and empathy, as the two are often confused. *Sympathy* is typically defined by feelings

FIGURE 8.2
Adaptation of the Lippitt-Knoster Model

Action Plan	+	Collective Efficacy	+	Goals	+	Formative Evaluation	+	Instructional Leadership	=	Change
Missing	+	Collective Efficacy	+	Goals	+	Formative Evaluation	+	Instructional Leadership	=	False Start
Action Plan	+	Missing	+	Goals	+	Formative Evaluation	+	Instructional Leadership	=	Fragmented Beliefs
Action Plan	+	Collective Efficacy	+	Missing	+	Formative Evaluation	+	Instructional Leadership	=	Reduced Motivation
Action Plan	+	Collective Efficacy	+	Goals	+	Missing	+	Instructional Leadership	=	Lack of Evidence
Action Plan	+	Collective Efficacy	+	Goals	+	Formative Evaluation	+	Missing	=	Confusion

of pity for another person, without really understanding what it's like to be in their situation. By contrast, *empathy* refers to the capacity or ability to imagine oneself in another's situation, experiencing the emotions, ideas, or opinions of that person.

What role does empathetic leadership play in the context of leading Achievement Teams? When teachers meet collaboratively using the Achievement Teams method, they should use formative assessment data to determine the success of their teaching. This process is, by nature, self-reflection and self-assessment. Teachers also use these data to determine instructional strategies to be implemented between a pre- and post-assessment. In many instances, the pre-assessment results do not always indicate high levels of proficiency, which is to be expected, especially if teachers are assessing new material. Nevertheless, pre-assessment results help teachers set and revise goals, identify students' strengths and weaknesses, and plan for corrective instruction.

This is when leaders need to tap into their empathy and consider the challenges teachers face. They need to go beyond simply encouraging teams to "do their best." Empathetic leadership—or cognitive empathy—is when leaders understand the thoughts of their teacher teams as they complete this process. They ask themselves, "If I were part of this team, what would I be thinking right now?" This type of empathetic perspective taking can contribute to positive relationships while creating an organizational culture that values the efforts and challenges others are experiencing. Without this perspective, leaders may miss signs of low morale or commitment and risk undermining teams' investment in collaborative problem solving (Brower, 2021).

A recent study found the following (O.C. Tanner, 2024):

- Sixty-one percent of employees surveyed (889 people) reported that they were more likely to be innovative under the guidance of an empathetic leader.
- Seventy-six percent reported that they were more engaged in work.
- In terms of retention, 57 percent of white women and 62 percent of women of color said they were unlikely to think of leaving their companies when they felt their life circumstances were respected and valued by their companies.
- Fifty percent of people with empathetic leaders reported that their workplace was inclusive, compared with only 17 percent of those with less empathetic leadership.

This highlights the strong correlation between empathy and relationship building, which results in a measurable boost in productivity and growth and makes the case for instructional leaders to reflect on their own levels of empathy and emotional intelligence.

If you are curious about your own level of empathy, you can experiment with the empathy quotient (EQ) tool located here: https://psychology-tools.com/test/empathy-quotient. This questionnaire was developed by Simon Baron-Cohen at the Autism Research Center at the University of Cambridge. After completing the questionnaire, you will receive an EQ score. It's important to note that this tool, despite its reference to autism, is also used to measure temperamental empathy among the general population (Baron-Cohen & Wheelwright, 2004).

✏️ **Empathy**

Think about your own experiences with empathy. Who is the most empathetic person you know? How does it make you feel to be around this person?

_____

_____

_____

_____

Leadership Pitfalls and How to Avoid Them

Missteps are part of the leadership experience, and the usual suspects are alive and well (e.g., miscommunication, complacency, lack of self-awareness, a noncollaborative environment). There is a strong correlation between leadership flaws or weaknesses and substandard performance in schools and districts. However, mistakes also provide opportunities for corrective leadership, and reflective leaders who recognize their missteps are not likely to repeat them.

The good news is that leaders can develop, refine, and improve their leadership capabilities. Macklin and Zbar (2020) describe the major contrasts between leaders who make things happen and those who cannot. These attributes consist of five skills and knowledge bases:

- Developing a shared narrative in the school, maximizing impact on students.
- Having expectations and promoting challenging goals for all.
- Providing supportive processes and structures to do the work.
- Being proficient in leading the collective to maximize impact.
- Knowing how to effectively implement, evaluate, and improve interventions throughout the school.

Attributes such as these assist leaders with their own vision, providing the opportunity to adapt to several different areas based on context. When leaders can isolate an area or areas needing improvement and then refer to these five areas, they have an advantage. This is not to suggest that leading schools and improving your leadership profile is simple, but when leaders refer to certain leadership criteria, it gives them something to reference as they refine and improve practice.

Overconfidence Bias

When teachers collaborate, there must be time to study student work, analyze assessment results, learn about instructional strategies, and reflect on teaching practices with an emphasis on improvement. Actions such as these collectively affect student achievement, while raising levels of trust and interdependence among the school community.

During my travels across the country, I have been privileged to observe and support teacher teams by providing specific feedback and guidance. In fact, a large part of my work involves realizing the advantages of high-functioning teacher teams by coaching them. Before I visit a school and coach their teams, I usually ask the building principal to give me an idea of how teachers are implementing Achievement Teams. To get an accurate depiction of teacher team success, I may ask the principal to use a simple reflection tool (Figure 8.3) as an overall indicator of implementation.

In many instances, principals report that teacher teams and collaborative protocols are common practice within the school. This would be considered a 5 on the scale in Figure 8.3 and means there is consistency with an emphasis on regularly implementing the Achievement Teams process. Once I begin coaching teams, I often notice gaps between the principal's assessment and the actual current reality of those teams. This type of overconfidence can impede the function of teacher teams and their actions because there is no accurate or objective measure to determine how well initiatives, such as PLCs, are being implemented.

FIGURE 8.3
Reflection Activity: Assessing Your Level of Collaboration

> Assess your current level of collaboration using the Likert scale below:
>
> 1--------2--------3--------4--------5
>
> 1 = Nonpracticing; This has not yet been established.
> 2 = Initial stages; We are starting to take action.
> 3 = Progressing; There are small pockets of success.
> 4 = Partial implementation, but this could not be considered common practice.
> 5 = This is common practice in our school.
>
> Explain why you gave yourself this rating. What has been established and is currently working? What are your biggest weaknesses in terms of collaboration?

Overconfidence bias has several consequences (MasterClass, 2022):

1. It can affect objective decision making.
2. It can artificially inflate the skills and abilities of you or others around you.
3. It can distort what should be commonsense reasoning.
4. It can lead to excessive confidence where one believes they are correct 90 percent of the time.

So, is overconfidence bias a good or bad thing? It depends. Success can absolutely increase one's self-confidence, which is a good thing. However, too much confidence may lead us to believe that we don't need to improve our practice.

Many times, I have witnessed overconfident building- and district-level leaders make decisions that were effective. These types of leaders tend to push for innovation, and they often possess the ability to convince others that they can overcome difficulties they originally believed were too challenging. Similarly, some leaders simply refuse to accept limitations.

By contrast, how often have you heard teachers or leaders claim, "We are already doing this"? Think about the principals who report that their teacher teams are functioning at high levels when, after careful review, they are not. This type of overconfidence prevents additional learning and can lead to inaccurate levels of overestimation. This not only affects collaboration but also spills over into many other crucial areas, such as instructional strategies, school climate, and equity and diversity.

So how can we reduce overconfidence bias? Optimism is an excellent leadership trait, but so is practicality. Overconfidence bias can often lead to uncompromising decision making. To diminish this, leaders can and should

- **Ask for feedback.** A good place to start is with your highest-performing people. You can ask them about how people perceive you and your message. If you have the confidence to ask, you will be able to raise your own level of awareness and self-reflection.
- **Practice humility.** If you are sincerely interested in leading an organization with positive influence and trust, then it would not be wise to act superior to the people you are leading. Being ambitious and self-assured are admirable leadership traits, but they should not be confused with simply telling others what to do. Humble leaders demonstrate the ability to lean on people for help without fearing others will perceive them as being "soft" or no longer in charge. You demonstrate emotional intelligence by managing your ego.
- **Consider your strengths and weaknesses objectively.** One of the best ways to practice self-reflection is by incorporating the use of a time reflection log where you list some of the leadership practices you would like to monitor, creating your own internal feedback loop (Figure 8.4). After completing your time reflection log each week, you can share the results with the rest of your team/staff, demonstrating your commitment to improving your leadership practices.
- **Use the adapted Lippitt-Knoster Model.** As previously demonstrated, my adaptation to this model is designed to help leaders avoid gaps while making certain that decisions are made based on evidence and not gut feelings.

FIGURE 8.4
Leadership Time Reflection Log

How much time did I spend doing the following tasks last week?	Time (in minutes)	Comments
Being highly visible around the school	47 minutes	I want to increase time spent in this area.
Attending PLCs/teacher team meetings		
Interpreting assessment results with teachers	32 minutes	I felt I added value to this activity.
Observing classrooms and instruction		
Participating in teacher learning and development		
	Total	
	79 minutes	

Sunk Cost Fallacy

This final section is about the sunk cost fallacy and how it can interfere with making rational decisions. There are numerous definitions and descriptions of this concept, but it is commonly understood to be an investment that is extremely difficult to recover. It occurs in every industry, including academia and education. In short, the sunk cost fallacy embodies our tendency to continue with an endeavor into which we've invested money, effort, or time—even if the current costs outweigh the benefits.

This practice causes normally rational people to disregard common sense, allowing past decisions to affect their future choices, despite seeing consistently poor results (Newlands, 2016). When viewed from a rational and objective perspective, it's obvious that we should "cut our losses" when necessary. However, what if there were a way to avoid getting involved with an investment that never seems to yield a positive return or gain? In education, that gain is almost always focused on increasing student levels of proficiency, school culture, and motivation.

Let's first imagine a scenario outside the educational context. Say you purchased a ticket to a very expensive concert—one you have been looking forward to for quite some time. Sadly, about 20 minutes into the concert you realize you made a mistake. You are not enjoying the concert, the music isn't very good, and the venue is quite uncomfortable. As with many concerts, your ticket was a nonrefundable investment. Rather than leave, though, you decide to stay for the entire two hours of the concert because you personally feel bad about wasting your money. This is called *loss aversion*, which can sometimes lead to irrational decision making.

Can you think of an educational decision made by your district or site leadership that never really materialized, despite an enormous cost? I know I can. I remember when a large school district decided to purchase an expensive software-driven item bank to help teachers with formative assessment and evaluation. Each teacher was issued a username and password to access the system. The district was required to purchase several license agreements to allow this access. After receiving training, the teachers were told to access the item bank and use it to assist with their collaborative team cycles. A few months into this investment, district-level administrators were interested in seeing who was using the tool. However, they were disappointed to discover that only 15 percent of teachers had logged into the system—and only a handful of those teachers actually created assessments. Rather than reassess the purchase, the district doubled down by purchasing additional licenses and training. They had developed an emotional attachment to their purchase, which prevented district-level leaders from stepping back and making a rational decision.

How can we overcome the sunk cost fallacy? An article from Facet (2023) suggests three actions:

1. **Zoom out.** We sometimes lose sight of reality when we have slipped in too deep. It's important to distinguish between important and unimportant investments using an outsider's point of view.
2. **Zoom in.** Use more objective decision making before investing in a program or service that may not materialize.
3. **Focus.** Acknowledge when decisions made are no longer beneficial.

Leaders can overcome the sunk cost fallacy by understanding the concept and its causes—and ensuring others on their team are on the same page. Cognitive biases tend to encourage irrational decision making, and in education, we are always looking for that "secret sauce" program that can help turn things around.

Leadership can enhance a school's or a district's culture, especially when leaders become skilled practitioners who lead with clarity and consistency. However, skilled leadership is a choice; leaders choose to be either average or exceptional. To lead collaborative team cycles and effective instruction, you must gather and prioritize what you consider to be the most prominent strategies from this book—then make a commitment to transfer those priorities to practice. If you have a passion to educate, without the need to learn, then you have a desire to hold a title, not to fulfill a purpose.

"What? So What? Now What?" Critical Reflection Model

What? In this chapter, we synthesized key leadership lessons necessary to enhance teacher collaboration:

1. Relationships between leadership vision and overall culture.
2. Strategies to develop and implement a shared vision.
3. Five focuses to help lead change, foster collaboration, and strengthen school teams (action planning, collective efficacy, goal setting, formative evaluation, instructional leadership).
4. The importance of leading with empathy.
5. Leadership pitfalls and how to avoid them.

It's one thing to have a road map to success, but the mindsets, traits, and qualities of a leader following that road map help determine if they reach their desired destination.

So What? What are the implications for this chapter and your leadership framework? What are the implications of the research?

_____

_____

_____

_____

Now What? What will you do differently as a result?

_____
_____
_____
_____

REFERENCES

Amobi, F. A., & Irwin, L. (2009). Implementing on-campus microteaching to elicit pre-service teachers' reflection on teaching actions: Fresh perspective on an established practice. *Journal of the Scholarship of Teaching and Learning, 9*(1), 27–34.

Bandura, A. (1989). Human agency in social cognitive theory. *American Psychologist, 44*(9), 1175–1184.

Barkley, S. (2024, July 27). Professional working communities and professional learning communities. Steve Barkley: Education Consultant. https://barkleypd.com/blog/professional-working-communities-and-professional-learning-communities

Baron-Cohen, S., & Wheelwright, S. (2004). The empathy quotient: An investigation of adults with Asperger Syndrome or high functioning autism, and normal sex differences. *Journal of Autism and Developmental Disorders, 34*(2), 163–175.

Black, P., & Wiliam, D. (1998). Assessment and classroom learning. *Assessment in Education: Principles, Policy & Practice, 5*(1), 7–74.

Bloom, B. S. (1968). Learning for mastery. Instruction and curriculum. Regional Education Laboratory for the Carolinas and Virginia, Topical Papers and Reprints, Number 1. *Evaluation Comment, 1*(2).

Borton. T. (1970). *Reach, touch, and teach: Student concerns and process education*. McGraw-Hill.

Brookfield, S. (1995). *Becoming a critically reflective teacher*. Jossey-Bass.

Brower, T. (2021). Empathy is the most important leadership skill according to research. *Forbes*. https://www.forbes.com/sites/tracybrower/2021/09/19/empathy-is-the-most-important-leadership-skill-according-to-research

Bryk, A., & Schneider, B. (2002). *Trust in schools: A core resource for improvement*. Russell Sage Foundation.

Cambridge International Education Teaching and Learning Team. (2019). *Getting started with reflective practice*. https://www.cambridge-community.org.uk/professional-development/gswrp/index.html

Caredda, S. (2020). Models: The Lippitt-Knoster Model for managing complex change. Sergio Caredda. https://sergiocaredda.eu/organisation/models-the-lippitt-knoster-model-for-managing-complex-change

Center for Leadership & Educational Equity. (2024). Atlas-learning from student work protocol. CLEE. https://www.clee.org/resources/atlas-learning-from-student-work-protocol

Chevallier, A., Dalsace, F., & Barsoux, J.-L. (2024). The art of asking smarter questions. *Harvard Business Review*. https://hbr.org/2024/05/the-art-of-asking-smarter-questions

Cohen, J. (1988). *Statistical power analysis for the behavioral sciences* (2nd ed.). Lawrence Erlbaum.

Cornell University. (2024). Collaborative learning. Center for Teaching Innovation. https://teaching.cornell.edu/teaching-resources/active-collaborative-learning/collaborative-learning

Doran, G. T. (1981). There's a S.M.A.R.T. way to write management's goals and objectives. *AMA Forum*, 35–36.

Dunst, C., Hamby, D., Howse, R., Wilkie, H., & Annas, K. (2019). Metasynthesis of preservice professional preparation and teacher education research studies. *Education Sciences, 9*(1), 50.

Dweck, C. S. (2016). *Mindset: The new psychology of success*. Random House.

Facet. (2023). Escaping the trap: What is the sunk cost fallacy, and how can I overcome it? https://facet.com/financial-wellness/escaping-the-trap-what-is-the-sunk-cost-fallacy-and-how-can-i-overcome-it

Finlay, L. (2008). Reflecting on "reflective practice." https://oro.open.ac.uk/68945/1/Finlay-%282008%29-Reflecting-on-reflective-practice-PBPL-paper-52.pdf

Fullan, M. (2008) *The six secrets of change: What the best leaders do to help their organizations survive and thrive*. Jossey-Bass.

Gentry, B. (2024). The importance of empathy in the workplace. Center for Creative Leadership. https://www.ccl.org/articles/leading-effectively-articles/empathy-in-the-workplace-a-tool-for-effective-leadership

Gibbs, G. (1988). *Learning by doing, a guide to teaching and learning methods*. https://stephenp.net/wp-content/uploads/2015/12/learning-by-doing-graham-gibbs.pdf

Goddard, R. (2002). Collective efficacy and school organization: A multilevel analysis of teacher influence in schools. *Theory and Research in Educational Administration, 1,* 169–184.

Goddard, R. D., Hoy, W. K., & Hoy, A. W. (2000). Collective teacher efficacy: Its meaning, measure, and effect on student achievement. *American Education Research Journal, 37*(2), 479–502.

Godin, S. (2008). *Tribes: We need you to lead us*. Portfolio.

Guskey, T. (2019). Grades versus comments: Research on student feedback. *Phi Delta Kappan, 101*(3), 42–47. https://tguskey.com/wp-content/uploads/Kappan-2019-Grades-versus-Comments.pdf

Guskey, T. (2023). *Implementing mastery learning* (3rd ed.). Corwin.

Hattie, J. (2009). *Visible learning: A synthesis of over 800 meta-analyses relating to achievement.* Routledge.

Hattie, J. (2012). *Visible learning for teachers: Maximizing impact on learning.* Routledge.

Hattie, J. (2015, July 13–14). *Keynote address* [Conference presentation]. 2015 Annual Visible Learning Plus Conference, San Antonio, TX.

Hattie, J. (2023). *Visible learning: The sequel*. Routledge.

Hattie, J., Fisher, D., & Frey, N. (2017). *Visible learning for mathematics, grades K–12: What works best to optimize student learning*. Corwin.

Hattie, J., & Zierer, K. (2018). *10 mindframes for visible learning: Teaching for success*. Routledge.

Hess, K. (2025). *Applying depth of knowledge and cognitive rigor: An educator's guide to supporting deeper learning.* Teachers College Press.

Hoy, A. W. (2000, April 28). Changes in teacher efficacy during the early years of teaching. Paper presented at the Annual Meeting of the American Educational Research Association, New Orleans, Lousiana.

Irwin, V. (2023). *Report on the condition of education 2023*. Institute of Education Sciences. https://nces.ed.gov/pubs2023/2023144.pdf

Jerald, C. D. (2007). *Believing and achieving.* Issue brief. Center for Comprehensive School Reform and Improvement. https://files.eric.ed.gov/fulltext/ED495708.pdf

Jitendra, A. K., Harwell, M. R., Dupuis, D. N., & Karl, S. R. (2016). A randomized trial of the effects of schema-based instruction on proportional problem-solving for students with mathematics problem-solving difficulties. *Journal of Learning Disabilities, 50*(3), 322–336.

Killion, J. (n.d.). The ten roles of coaches. Pennsylvania Association of Career & Technical Administrators. https://pacareertech.org/content_documents/9/TheTenRolesofCoaches.pdf

Kirtman, L. (2013). *Leadership and teams: The missing piece of the education reform puzzle.* Pearson Education.

Klint, A. (2021, October 21). Understanding Depth of Knowledge. Renaissance. https://www.renaissance.com/2021/10/21/blog-understanding-depth-of-knowledge

Knight, J. (2013). *Focus on teaching: Using video for high-impact instruction.* Corwin.

Knight, J. (2019). Instructional coaching for implementing visible learning: A model for translating research into practice. *Education Sciences, 9*(2), 101.

Lang-Raad, N. (2025). *The AI assist: Strategies for integrating AI into the very human act of teaching.* ASCD.

Macklin, P., & Zbar, V. (2020). *Driving school improvement: Practical strategies and tools* (2nd ed.). ACER.

MasterClass. (2022). What is overconfidence bias? 3 types of overconfidence bias. https://www.masterclass.com/articles/overconfidence-bias

Murphy, J., & Hallinger, P. (1988). Characteristics of instructionally effective school districts. *Journal of Educational Research, 81*(3), 175–181.

Newlands, M. (2016). What the 1996 Everest disaster teaches about leadership. *Entrepreneur.* https://www.entrepreneur.com/leadership/what-the-1996-everest-disaster-teaches-about-leadership/283197

O.C. Tanner. (2024). Empathy in action: What does it mean to be an empathetic leader? https://www.octanner.com/articles/empathetic-leadership-qualities

Otsupius, I. (2014). Micro-teaching: A technique for effective teaching. *African Research Review, 8*(4), 183.

Peker, M. (2009). The use of expanded microteaching for reducing pre-service teachers' teaching anxiety about mathematics. *Scientific Research and Essay, 4*(9), 872–880.

Pilotti, M., Anderson, S., Hardy, P., Murphy, P., & Vincent, P. (2017). Factors related to cognitive, emotional, and behavioral engagement in the online asynchronous classroom. *International Journal of Teaching and Learning in Higher Education, 29*(1), 145–153.

Prieur, J. (2022, June 23). 9 high-yield research-based instructional strategies and how I would use them. Prodigy. https://www.prodigygame.com/main-en/blog/research-based-instructional-strategies

Reeves, D., Frey, N., & Fisher, D. (2022). *Confronting the crisis of engagement: Creating focus and resilience for students, staff, and communities.* Corwin.

Robinson, V. M. J., Lloyd, C. A., & Rowe, K. J. (2008). The impact of leadership on student outcomes: An analysis of the differential effects of leadership types. *Educational Administration Quarterly, 44*(5), 635–674.

Rohrer, D., & Pashler, H. (2007). Increasing retention without increasing study time. *Current Directions in Psychological Science, 16*(4), 183–186.

Schmoker, M. (1999). *Results: The key to continuous school improvement* (2nd ed.). ASCD.

Stern, J., Ferraro, K., Duncan, K., & Aleo, T. (2021). *Learning that transfers: Designing curriculum for a changing world.* Corwin.

Sweeney, D., & Harris, L. S. (2020). *The essential guide for student-centered coaching.* Corwin.

Trist, E., & Murray, H. (Eds.). (1990). *The social engagement of social science: A Tavistock anthology.* University of Pennsylvania Press.

Turing, A. (1950). Computing machinery and intelligence. *Mind, 59*(236), 433–460.

Ventura, S. (2024). Common PLC pitfalls . . . and how to fix them. Advanced Collaborative Solutions. https://www.steveventura.com/blog/common-plc-pitfalls-and-how-to-fix-them

Ventura, S., & Ventura, M. (2022). *Achievement Teams: How a better approach to PLCs can improve student outcomes and teacher efficacy.* ASCD.

WalkMe Team. (2024). Managing complex change with the Lippitt-Knoster Model. https://www.walkme.com/blog/managing-complex-change

INDEX

The letter *f* following a page locator denotes a figure and *qrc* indicates a QR Code.

accountability in leadership, 2, 4–5, 24–25
achievement
    leaders impact on, 64
    mindframes of, 70–71
Achievement Teams
    AI used with, 120
    coaching, 51–52, 57, 65
    data discussions model, 85*f*
    data discussions steps, 85–87, 87*f*
    essential actions, 91*f*
    focus of, 62
    instructional strategy play card, 39, 40*f*
    leadership checklist, 93–95
    overconfidence bias, 132–134
    process, 71
    purpose of, 38, 84
    success criteria, 73–74*f*
Achievement Teams collaboration, elements of effective
    informed decision making using data from, 83–87
    lead change in PLCs, 90–92
    monitoring plan, 68, 69*f*
    relational trust, 87–90
    understanding that instructional effort is reflected in assessment, 75–78, 80–83
    a well-defined structure, 68, 70–71
Achievement Teams protocol, 38–39, 38*f*, 71–72, 73*f*, 110, 113–119
action plans in change implementation, 127, 129*f*

artificial intelligence (AI)
    Achievement Teams using, 113–119
    concerns surrounding use of, 109, 119–120
    defined, 108
    ethical and responsible use of, 119–120
    short-cycle assessment using, 111–113
assessment
    connecting to instruction, 90–92, 91*f*
    depth of knowledge, 80, 81*f*
    grading, 82–83
    informed decision making using data from, 83–87
    instructional effort reflected in results of, 75–78
    post-assessment measures, 92–93, 93*f*
    pre-assessments, 90–91, 93*f*
    short-cycle using AI, 111–113
assessment cycle, 93*f*
assessment strategy analysis, 76–78

baseline evidence statements, 38*f*, 71, 73*f*, 83–84, 110, 117–118

Caton School, 106–107
celebrations, 4, 94
challenge, engagement and, 37
change, components for implementing, 126–128, 129*f*
clarity, leadership, 2–3, 24–25
class discussion strategy, 34*f*, 46
coaches, role of, 55

coaching
    Achievement Teams, 51–52, 57, 65
    impact, leaders in maximizing, 64
    purpose of, 57
coaching, stages of
    identify, 58–59
    improve, 58, 61–62
    learn, 58, 59–61
coaching effect sizes
    on learning attitudes, 54–55, 54f
    overall, 53–54
    on self-efficacy beliefs, 54f, 56
    on skill acquisition, 54f, 57
    on teaching practice, 54f, 57
collaboration
    engagement and, 37
    successful, requirements for, 5, 7
collaboration, elements of effective
    informed decision making using data from, 83–87
    lead change in PLCs, 90–92
    monitoring plan, 68, 69f
    relational trust, 87–90
    supportive leadership, 5
    understanding that instructional effort is reflected in assessment, 5, 75–78, 80–83
    a well-defined structure, 5, 68, 70–71
collective, 1, 2–5
collective efficacy
    in change implementation, 127, 129f
    teachers, 56
communication in leadership, 94
community in an instructional leadership vision, 7
concept mapping strategy, 34f, 46
conceptual knowledge, transforming strategy, 35f, 47
consistency in leadership, 2–4
content chunking instructional strategy, 31
coordinating, effective leadership role in, 17, 18f
critical reflection model, 9–10, 9f
culture, leadership in creating, 123
curriculum, effective leadership role in, 17, 18f

data
    in the assessment cycle, 92–93, 93f
    collect and chart protocol, 38f, 71, 73f, 83, 110
    collect and chart using AI, 113–114
    for informed decision making, 83–87
data collection form, 114qrc
data discussions model, 85f
data discussions steps, 85–87, 87f
data-driven discussions, 94

decision making
    data for informed, 83–87
    irrational, 136
    sunk cost fallacy, overcoming the, 136–137
deep learning instructional strategies, 31–32, 34f, 46–47
depth of knowledge, 78, 79f, 80–81, 81f, 82f
detail wheel, 60f
discussion, data-driven, 94
distributed practice instructional strategy, 30

education, role of instructional strategies in, 28–29
empathy, leading with, 128–130
engagement
    emotional, 37
    improving, methods of, 37
    instructional leaders influence on, 32, 37
    success criteria and, 59–60, 60f
environment
    to improve school outcomes, 21f, 23, 24f
    leadership in ensuring an orderly and supportive, 17, 18f
expectations, effective leadership in establishing, 16, 18f

feedback
    diminishing overconfidence bias, 134
    improving, 59
    leadership trait of, 94
    learning labs and, 100–101, 103–106, 104f
    microteaching and, 99
Find Someone Activity graphic organizer, 48, 48–49f
formative assessment
    in change implementation, 127–128, 129f
    data, using for informed decision making, 83–87
    effective, 75–78
    grading and, 82–83
Formative Assessment Planning Template, 77f, 81f

Gibbs Reflective Cycle, 23, 24f
goals
    in change implementation, 127, 129f
    effective leadership in establishing, 16, 18f
    in an instructional leadership vision, 7
grading assessments, 82–83
growth mindset, 55

humility, diminishing overconfidence bias, 134

identify coaching stage, 58–59
implementation, tracking, monitoring, and adjusting, 25–26

improve coaching stage, 58, 61–62
improvement, organizational structures fostering, 123, 125
instruction
  direct, 39
  teacher-led, 39
instructional decision making, data for informed, 83–87
instructional practice, coaching effect size, 54*f*, 57
instructional strategies
  content chunking, 31
  deep learning, 31–32, 34*f*, 46–47
  distributed practice, 30
  domains of, 41
  fostering the use of, 29–31
  high-yield, selecting in Achievement teams, 38*f*, 71, 73*f*, 110
  high-yield, selecting using AI, 118–119
  massed practice, 30
  research-based, 28
  role in education, 28–29
  selecting, 30
  spaced practice, 30
  surface learning, 31–32, 33*f*, 46
  transfer learning, 35*f*, 47
Instructional Strategy Flipbook
  described, 39*qrc*
  Find Someone Activity graphic organizer, 48, 48–49*f*
  link to, 39*qrc*
  play card, 39, 40*f*
  Surface, Deep, and Transfer Matrix application, 47–48
  using the, 42–45
interpretive questions, 63*f*
investigative questions, 63*f*

labor peace, 123, 125
leadership
  accountability in, 2, 4–5, 24–25
  achievement, impact on, 64
  in action, 15–16
  beliefs about, reflecting on, 124*f*
  in change implementation, 128, 129*f*
  clarity in, 2–3, 24–25
  coaches impact, maximizing, 64
  collective, maximizing impact with, 5
  consistency in, 2–4
  content, examples of, 8
  effective, 2, 4, 8, 12–13, 16–19, 18*f*, 64
  empathetic, 128–130
  exceptional, 2, 4
  inspirational, 3
  instructional impact, acquiring, 25

leadership (*continued*)
  mindsets, 14
  organizational, example of, 8
  pitfalls, avoiding, 131–132
  thinking prompts, 68, 70
  tracking and monitoring initiative implementation, 25–26
  visionary, 2, 7–9, 123, 126–128
Leadership Anticipation Guide, 124*f*
leadership framework to improve school outcomes, 20–21, 21*f*, 23–25, 24*f*
Leadership Time Reflection Log, 135*f*
learn coaching stage, 58, 59–61
learning
  collaborative, 41
  cooperative, engagement and, 37
  deep, 31–32, 34*f*, 36*f*
  factual, 31
  microteaching effect size on, 98–99, 99*f*
  reflecting on, 41
  surface, 36*f*
  surface-level, 31–32, 33*f*
  transfer, 35*f*, 36*f*
learning attitudes, coaching effect size, 54–55, 54*f*
learning environment
  orderly and supportive, effective leaders role in ensuring, 17, 18*f*
  reflective, 21*f*, 23, 24*f*
learning intentions, 58–59, 61
Learning Lab Feedback Form, 104*f*, 103–106
learning labs
  advantages of, 101
  feedback and, 101, 103–106, 104*f*
  in action, 106–107
  introduction, 97
  setting up, 101–102
  successful, 102–103
Lippitt-Knoster Model, 126, 129*f*, 134
loss aversion, 136

management vs. leadership, 4
massed practice instructional strategy, 30
metacognition, 32
metacognition strategy, 34*f*, 46
microteaching
  benefits of, 58, 100
  effect size, 98–99, 99*f*
  feedback and, 99
  to improve professional learning, 57
  introduction, 97
microteaching cycle, 99–100, 100*f*
mindframes of achievement, 70–71
mindset, instructional leaders, 14

mistakes, accepting, 37
motivation, instructional leaders' influence on, 32, 37

note taking strategy, 33*f*, 46

outlining strategy, 33*f*, 46
overconfidence bias, 132–134

peer tutoring strategy, 35*f*, 47
planning, effective leaders role in, 17, 18*f*
pluralistic ignorance, 62
pre-assessments, 90–91, 93*f*
pre-teaching, 90–91
problem-solving teaching strategy, 35*f*, 47
productive questions, 63*f*
productivity focus for improvement, 125
professional learning, microteaching to improve, 57
professional learning communities (PLCs)
    leader participation in, 4
    leadership checklist, 93–95
    leading change for exceptional, 90
    pitfalls, avoiding, 52–53
    purpose of coaching, 57
    using AI with, 120

questioning techniques, 62–64, 63*f*
question stems, surface, deep, and transfer learning, 36*f*

reciprocal teaching strategy, 34*f*, 47
reflection
    critical reflection model, 9–10, 9*f*
    on leadership beliefs, 124*f*
    Leadership Time Reflection Log, 135*f*
    leadership trait of, 94
    on learning, 41
Relational Trust Scale, 87–88, 89*f*
relationships, empathy and, 130
resourcing, effective leaders role in, 17, 18*f*, 94

safety, emotional, 37
school outcomes, leadership framework to improve, 20–21, 21*f*, 23–25, 24*f*

self-efficacy, coaching effect size, 54*f*, 56
self-reflection, 23, 32, 98, 134
self-reflective questions, 64
similarities and differences, identifying strategy, 35*f*, 47
skill acquisition, coaching effect size, 54*f*, 57
SMART goals, 38*f*, 71, 73*f*, 110, 114–116
spaced practice instructional strategy, 30
speculative questions, 63*f*
students, building independence, 41
success, celebrating, 94
success criteria, 59–61, 60*f*
summarizing strategy, 33*f*, 46
sunk cost fallacy, 135–137
support, leadership trait of, 94
Surface, Deep, and Transfer Matrix
    Flipbook application, 47–48
    instructional strategies, 33–35*f*
surface learning instructional strategies, 31–32, 33*f*, 46
sympathy vs. empathy, 128–129

teachers
    assessment, effective leaders and, 17, 18*f*
    collaboration, indicators of effective, 5, 7
    learning and development, effective leaders role in, 17, 18*f*
teachers, coaching
    instructional practice and, 54*f*, 57
    learning attitudes and, 54–55, 54*f*
    self-efficacy and, 54*f*, 56
    skill acquisition and, 54*f*, 57
teaching, reflective, 23, 24*f*, 64
thinking maps strategy, 34*f*, 46
transfer learning, defined, 45–46
transfer learning instructional strategies, 35*f*, 47
trust, relational, 87–90

video. *See* microteaching
vision
    clarity in, 3
    shared, developing and implementing a, 126–128
visionary leadership, 2, 7–9, 123, 126–128
vocabulary instruction strategy, 33*f*, 46

ABOUT THE AUTHOR

 **Steve Ventura** is the president and lead consultant at Advanced Collaborative Solutions. A highly motivational and knowledgeable speaker, he brings practical, research-based strategies to high-stakes professional development. Steve's experience includes roles as an elementary and secondary teacher and as a school and district-level administrator. He has authored multiple books and articles and is a frequent presenter and keynote speaker at global education events. Steve is passionate about helping school-based leaders build a culture of collective efficacy through his flagship work, Achievement Teams, which has supported countless educators in enhancing their teaching practice.

Related ASCD Resources: Instructional Leadership

At the time of publication, the following resources were available (ASCD stock numbers in parentheses).

Achievement Teams: How a Better Approach to PLCs Can Improve Student Outcomes and Teacher Efficacy by Steve Ventura and Michelle Ventura (#122034)

Building a Strong Foundation: How School Leaders Can Help New Teachers Succeed and Stay by Michelle Hope (#124015)

Embracing MESSY Leadership: How the Experience of 20,000 School Leaders Can Transform You and Your School by Alyssa Gallagher and Rosie Connor (#124011)

Highly Effective PLCs and Teacher Teams (Quick Reference Guide) by Steve Ventura and Michelle Ventura (#QRG123050)

Illuminate the Way: The School Leader's Guide to Addressing and Preventing Teacher Burnout by Chase Mielke (#123032)

Make Your School Irresistible: The Secret to Attracting and Retaining Great Teachers by Jessica Holloway and Carrie Bishop (#124012)

School Culture Rewired: Toward a More Positive and Productive School for All, 2nd Edition by Steve Gruenert and Todd Whitaker (#123029)

What Can I Take Off Your Plate? A Structural—and Sustainable—Approach to Countering Teacher Burnout by Jill Handley and Lara Donnelly (#125002)

For up-to-date information about ASCD resources, go to www.ascd.org. You can search the complete archives of *Educational Leadership* at www.ascd.org/el.

For more information, send an email to member@ascd.org; call 1-800-933-2723 or 703-578-9600; send a fax to 703-575-5400; or write to Information Services, ASCD, 2111 Wilson Boulevard, Suite 300, Arlington, Virginia 22201, USA.

Transform Instruction to
Transform Students' Lives

iste+ascd

Our Transformational Learning Principles (TLPs) are evidence-based practices that ensure students have access to high-impact, joyful learning experiences.

Endorsed by AASA and NASSP, the TLPs provide a shared language and a framework for reimagining teaching and learning, focusing on nurturing student growth, guiding intellectual curiosity, and empowering learners to take ownership of their education.

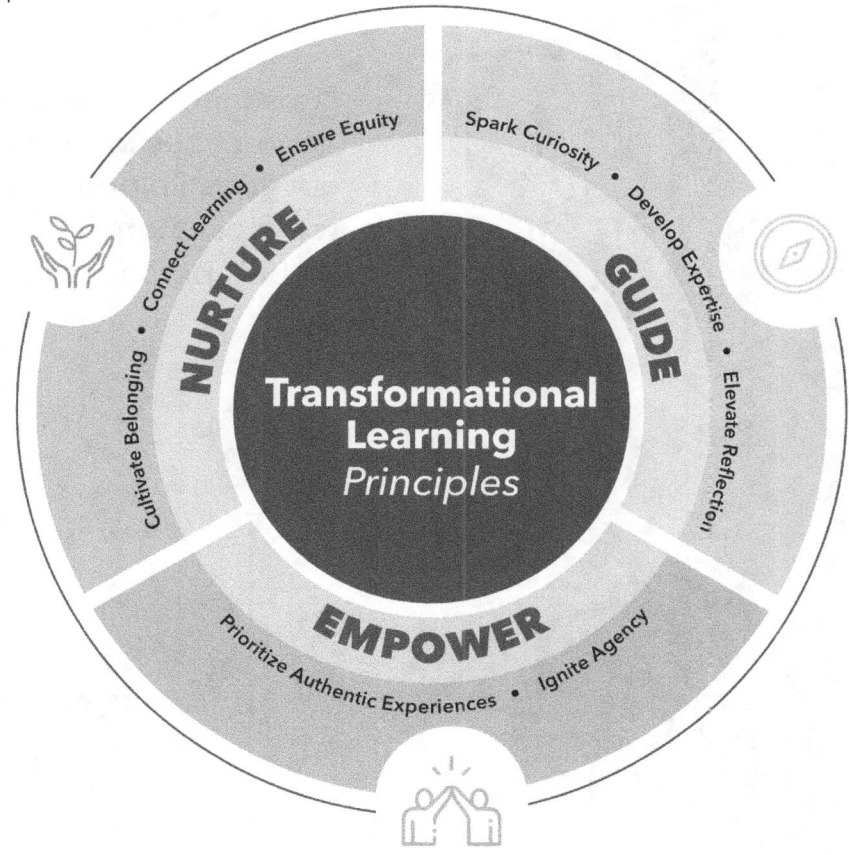

Learn more at **ascd.org/tlps**

DON'T MISS A SINGLE ISSUE OF THIS AWARD-WINNING MAGAZINE.

iste+ascd
educational leadership

If you belong to a Professional Learning Community, you may be looking for a way to get your fellow educators' minds around a complex topic. Why not delve into a relevant theme issue of *Educational Leadership*, the journal written by educators for educators?

Subscribe now and browse or purchase back issues of our flagship publication at **www.ascd.org/el**. Discounts on bulk purchases are available.

iste+ascd

Arlington, VA USA
1-800-933-2723

www.ascd.org
www.iste.org

www.ingramcontent.com/pod-product-compliance
Lightning Source LLC
Chambersburg PA
CBHW060538010526
44119CB00052B/751